"I love this devotional book that goes from being a devotional (a book) to devotions (the heartbeat of the book). While the theme is sports, it goes beyond the physical activities to the spiritual activities of the heart. As a martial artist I appreciate the correlation of the art of self-defense in the spiritual realm. Well done, Tammy."

Rodney Boyd, 2nd degree Black Belt
Author of *Never Run a Dead Kata*

"Tammy Chandler offers readers a fresh, insightful perspective on how to see God in various sports settings—individual, team, recreational, traditional, and water. She even encourages us through the equipment bags."

Cher Younger, ATC-L, Athletic Trainer

"Having picked up many devotionals throughout the years, honestly speaking, very few have captivated me enough where I looked forward to picking it up the next day. Reading through **Devotions from Every Day Sports** I found myself cheating. Tammy's ability to connect different sports activities to my personal spiritual development had me reading ahead. My initial intent was to see the next day's topic. Instead I found myself reading through several devotions at a time. This devotional is simple to read, yet triggered depth of thought in a way that helped me receive scriptures I've studied for years in a new way. Even the days where I feel like I'm running at 90 mph, taking a few moments to read and reflect on each devotion helped align my heart with the Lord, take a breath, and be ready for the race we call life."

David Simard, Sports Enthusiast

Devotions

from Everyday Sports

Enjoy!

Tammy Chandler

1 Corinthians 9:24

Devotions from Everyday Sports
Copyright © 2019
Tammy Chandler

ISBN: 978-1-948679-41-1

Published by WordCrafts Press
Cody, Wyoming 82414
www.wordcrafts.net

Devotions
from Everyday Sports

Tammy Chandler

WordCrafts

For my friends and family, who have shown me the world of sports—how to play, how to laugh, and how to see the world in a different light.

Love you all!

Contents

FOREWORD

After our middle son graduated from high school, he asked me when I was going to write a book about his interests, and ***Devotions from Everyday Sports*** was born. From that first conversation, I began to draw back the curtain on memories, as we had spent hours and hours at the ball fields, courts, and gymnasiums with our children as they were growing up. I started watching sports in our own backyard with a different perspective, and had lots of fun with friends, as I explored new games and learned new things about traditional ones.

Devotions from Everyday Sports is a labor of love, born out of a request from my son. I hope you enjoy reading it, as much as I did writing it. As we meditate on the spiritual concepts that sports can bring out in our lives, I pray we will apply Scripture to our situations, and compassion to our competitions. I look forward to working through these sports concepts with you, and I am praying for you. Enjoy the game.

PREFACE

D_evotions from Everyday Sports_ is a continuation of the
Devotions from Everyday Things series. Each book is a sixty-day
journey in which you will find spiritual truths illustrated in
ordinary things. An uncomplicated approach toward helping
you on your journey to finding deeper spiritual truths as you
notice how God is at work in the world around you.

How to use this book: The devotions are uncomplicated,
straightforward, quiet times with God. Each one contains a
daily Scripture passage, an illustration connected with a sport,
or a sports object, a Thought-provoker, and a Prayer Starter.
The Scripture passage allows us to see where the connection
is through God's Word; the illustration will help us to apply
the principles of Scripture to something we can take with us
throughout the day. The Thought-provoker is an opportunity
to adjust our thoughts or actions to the principles learned from
the devotion; it is also a great start for journaling or family
conversation. The Prayer Starter is a short conversation starter
about the topic of the devotion. It is an opportunity to thank
God for what we are learning, and to ask Him for the strength
we need to apply Biblical principles to our hearts and lives. It
is also a time for us to share our burdens and pour out our
hearts about personal struggles we are facing.

You can also join me at my blog site:

www.simplydevotions.wordpress.com

Thank you for joining me for this spiritual work out through ***Devotions from Everyday Sports.*** I am so excited you have chosen this book, and I am praying for you to know God in a richer way because you have chosen to learn more about the deep things in the game of life. Let's get started.

ACKNOWLEDGMENTS

To my Home Team—John, Jonathan, Jordan, and Charity— thank you for allowing me to share our lives with others through my writings. To our parents, and our extended family, thank you for your prayers as I write, and for sharing so many copies with your friends. You all continue to amaze me with your encouragement and support.

To our sports friends—thank you for the friendly competitions as I learned about new games, rules and sports for this book. Your patience, laughter, and friendship through this process have been a wonderful part of the process that I cherish in heartfelt memories.

To our Lighthouse family—I am so thankful for you all as you stood with me in prayer, encouraged me to keep going, and walked with me every step of the way. We are so blessed to be a part of such a strong, loving church family.

To the publishing team at WordCrafts Press—thank you for the privilege to be a part of the WordCrafts family, and for believing a fifth book was possible. Mike, Paula and the team—you are amazing!

To God our Father—Who knew each word before it was ever written on the page, to You be the honor and the glory for the great things You have done.

SIGN UPS

"But exhort one another daily, while it is called 'Today,'
lest any of you be hardened through the deceitfulness of sin."
Hebrews 3:13

Whether it is your Uncle Tommy saying, "Let's go shoot some hoops" at the family reunion, or it is an official sign up station at the gym, each of us have to sign up to get involved in sports. We cannot play sports by sitting on the sidelines and being spectators. In order to be athletes, either in the backyard or on the field, we have to sign up, step out, and commit to playing.

Each of us is called to sign up for the spiritual sports. From the moment we decide to put our faith and trust in the finished work of Christ on the cross, until the day we rest in our final victory in Heaven, we have to decide to be in the game of Christian growth. As we learn the guidelines, build our faith, follow His commands in baptism, evangelism and discipleship, we stay in the game. Each of us is invited to find our position on the team and to strive for victory.

This is your invitation. This is your sign up. Whether you are brand new to the game, or a seasoned veteran, it is time for us all to commit to being all-in. We need to examine ourselves, see what kind of spiritual shape we are in, and get ready to be the committed players we are asked to be in the kingdom of God. We need to exhort each other to stay in, to daily challenge each other to play the game of life with God's guidelines and His perspectives. He wants us to be a team that moves mountains, takes the Gospel to others, meets needs, and has good sportsmanship—His sportsmanship—in the game of life. He says to do it, "Today."

So, as we embark on this sixty-day challenge to learn spiritual truths from the sports around us, I want to encourage you to get in the game. If you are already playing hard and working intensely, catch your breath and renew your purpose. If you've been sitting tentatively on the sidelines, take a breath and jump in. Get moving for the glory of God and let Him guide you into the truths we can find in the games around us. Together, we will find challenges, refreshment and purpose in the recreational and competitive times we have in our lives. Sign up!

THOUGHT-PROVOKER:

As we embark on this challenge, where do we need to sign up, or re-commit, spiritually? Are we in good condition, or are we finding ourselves out of shape and sitting? Are we ready to see the spiritual truths in the games around us?

Lord, thank You that all things in life—even sports and recreation—have spiritual meanings for those who choose to see them. Help each of us to find direction, correction and encouragement in these pages in the coming days. In Jesus' name, Amen.

NOTES/INSIGHTS:

MINIATURE GOLF

"For now we see in a mirror, dimly, but then face to face. Now I know in part, but then I shall know just as I also am known."

1 Corinthians 13:12

We had a tradition when the kids were younger, that whenever we got together with their cousins over the summer at the beach, we would go play miniature golf. The miniature golf place was just across the street from the hotel, and it had tunnels, bridges and big rocks throughout the course—great places to get pictures of the cousins together and enjoy an activity. All of us—sometimes thirty in number—would head over for a time of fun and laughter as a family.

Miniature golf is a great activity for a family with a big age spread—it's not too long for the little ones, and it's not too difficult for the more mature family members to maneuver. But, it is also a miniature version of the real game of golf. The greens are much shorter, there are no long fairways to maneuver, and there is not near as much walking on a miniature golf course as there is on a golf course. Miniature golf gives us a glimpse of what regular golf is like.

This life is a miniature course of what our relationship with Christ is going to look like in eternity. Just like with our family, we will be together with those we love who have accepted the redeeming gift of grace Christ provided on the cross. This life shows us that Christ's offer is for everyone—young, old, or in-between—and everyone can join in. We get glimpses of what it will be like to talk with Him, walk with Him, be able to stand beside Him and perhaps, even take a family photo in Heaven with Him. The days we hit a hole-in-one as we are walking in the Spirit, and the days we totally miss par and hit the ball into the bushes—both give us an idea of the grace and mercy that await us when we see Him face to face.

So, while we trek through this miniature version of the real life that is to come, let's not forget to enjoy those around us, take time for those relationships, and catch the glimpses God is giving of us of the life we will have when we are all in His presence and enjoying the real version of eternal life offered by His nail-pierced hands. Look for those around you who should be joining us on that eternal journey, and share the news of the gift Christ has for them so they can become part of the family and join us for both the miniature version here, and the eternal version to come.

THOUGHT-PROVOKER:

Have we seen glimpses of the eternal life in our here and now? Are we grateful for those moments, and are we sharing them with others so they can join in?

Lord, thank You for the miniature version of the true, eternal life we will have with You in Heaven someday soon. Help us to share Your gift with others so they can join in too. In Jesus' name, Amen.

NOTES/INSIGHTS:

KICKBALL

"By this all will know that you are My disciples, if you have love for one another."

John 13:34-35

There is a sound familiar to almost everyone who took Physical Education classes in elementary school. There is a certain sound that only red, rubber kick balls make when they are kicked, or caught. It's that "*ker-thunk*" sound as the rubber absorbs the impact and the runner makes a sprint to first base. I remember year after year, in the early spring, we would be so excited to be able to go back outside after a long winter and play kickball against the other classes. It became a friendly rivalry as we would play week after week, and, of course, we kept track of runs, wins, and losses. I do not remember the names of all my teammates through the years, but I surely remember that sound of the ball.

That sound—knowing what it was, what it meant, is a piece of my childhood. It was distinct, unmistakable—unique and memorable. Even years later, it still touches a memory and makes me smile. Christ's love, demonstrated by believers, is supposed to be like that—a distinction that sets us apart from the humdrum of the world's selfishness. Christ's love flowing from us into the lives of others is an unmistakable mark we can make on the world. It is what makes us unique as Christ followers. It's what makes an impression—and makes memories—in the lives of those around us. Do we want to change our neighborhood? Start by loving our neighbors with the love of Christ. It probably won't be big, miraculous events—it will be just like coming up to the plate in a kickball game. We did it over and over again. On a few rare occasions, we were able to sail the ball over the heads of our opponents, but most of the time, we kicked it enough to get to first base. That's what Christ-love looks like—small acts of kindness, unselfishness, and generosity that change the way people see love. The kid in the neighborhood who is always in the street when we pull out, do we take the time to stop and talk with him for a few minutes, or are we too busy? The lady who lost her husband, do we check in on her from time-to-time and see what needs she has? Working together, one need at a time, we make the impact, and the distinct sound of Christ's love is heard in the game of life. Take those moments to share His love with others; be the red, rubber ball memory in their lives today.

THOUGHT-PROVOKER:

What "*ker-thunk*" will we make with Christ's love today? What distinct act of love on our part will point others to Christ now?

Lord, thank You that Your love is distinct, unmistakable, unique and memorable. Help us to give it away freely today to help others see You in this world. In Jesus' name, Amen.

Notes/Insights:

THE SOFTBALL GAME

"But you will receive power when the Holy Spirit has come upon you, and you will be my witnesses in Jerusalem and in all Judea and Samaria, and to the end of the earth."

Acts 1:8, ESV

Our two sons play on a men's softball team with our church. While it is not the same as the fast-pitch baseball style played in high school, we still have a good time going and watching them play, cheering in the stands, and catching up with the other church members who come to watch.

Last night as we watched, I noticed something about the softball strategy. If everyone hit the ball to the exact same spot on the field, the game would be boring and the other team would be able to make easy plays for outs. But, when each player hits the ball to a different area, the game picks up, runs are scored and the game becomes more exciting. Each player has been chosen to hit to a designated area by the coach. It may not work out perfectly on the ball field, but the coach guides the players with a "hit it out of the park" or "all we need is a base hit."

Missions is a lot like the softball strategy. If all we did as a church is hit the ball out of the park, foreign mission work, our opponent and enemy, would easily figure out how to stop our strategy. If we only did local work close to home, he would also figure out how to discourage us and how to slow the game. But, when each of us follows the leading of the Holy Spirit to cover the entire playing field, the game becomes exciting. As one player hits it over the fence and heads to the foreign field, and the next player opens a homeless shelter close to home, and another supports a ministry in the next town over, and still another starts an organization that links church members with mission's ministries, we all win. The team members use their strengths and resources, and the runs start piling up, as God brings new family members into His Kingdom. Hearts and souls are touched and changed by His grace and for His glory. We each have the ability to be in the game; we each have a place to minister.

So, where are you best equipped to serve? And the best question to ask—what is the Coach asking of you today? Let's stop making the game boring and find out where we can best serve to strengthen the Kingdom and win the game—the world is waiting for the Gospel and we are getting close to the final inning. Let's get in the game.

THOUGHT-PROVOKER:

Are we willing to accept the play He has for us in His world reaching strategy? Where is He sending us today? Will you go?

Father, thank You for allowing us the privilege of being part of Your team. Help us to hear Your leading today, and to go where You want us to go. Help each of us realize we have a part in Your strategy to reach a lost and hopeless world. In Jesus' name, Amen.

NOTES/INSIGHTS:

BADMINTON

"But also for this very reason, giving all diligence, add to your faith virtue, to virtue knowledge, to knowledge self-control, to self-control perseverance, to perseverance godliness, to godliness brotherly kindness, and to brotherly kindness love. For if these things are yours and abound, you will be neither barren nor unfruitful in the knowledge of our Lord Jesus Christ."

2 Peter 1:5-8

Almost every backyard celebration I remember as a child included a Badminton court. Some of my favorite memories of those times include shuttlecocks, i.e., birdies, landing on someone's picnic plate or, on rare occasions when my cousins and I were really good shots—splashing into someone's plastic cup on the picnic table.

The shuttlecock is an interesting projectile. Because of how it is made, it is not stable in the air. It soars rapidly up, but it also drops quickly. It loses momentum as it travels, and players have to know how to anticipate the fall in order to make a good play.

Players also have to have self-control. One of the disadvantages caused by the shuttlecock is that a strong whack with a racquet does not usually result in scored points. Hitting it too hard causes the shuttlecock to fly even more erratically, and it typically lands outside the field of play, or putters above the opponent's side, giving them a chance to defend and strike it in a downward motion on the other side of the net for a point.

So, what does Badminton teach us about our spiritual journey? It's a process. First, we desire to play the game, we then learn the guidelines of how to play it. After that, we choose a racquet and we start to play. We probably aren't very good, at first, but we keep at it; we learn new techniques and we add some finesse as we go along. At about this time, we may start to become impatient, and that's when we must remember to add self-control. If we keep our composure and play with the knowledge and skills we have learned, we keep making progress. We keep moving forward toward godliness. While Badminton may not be a spiritually-minded game, it does remind us of the process listed in our passage today. First, we give diligence to our faith. The faith that saved us—our trust in the work of Jesus Christ on the cross—keeps us. We then add virtue, in sports terms that is good sportsmanship. Next, we add knowledge; we learn the rules and guidelines to play the game well. Then comes self-control and perseverance—we learn to use our strength wisely and we don't quit the game. We then develop godliness, and that brings about brotherly kindness. It doesn't happen overnight, but as we keep playing, we will score points for the kingdom, and make good memories along the way.

Thought-provoker:

What spiritual shuttlecock are we swatting at today? Are we making spiritual progress, or are we short-circuiting the process with our lack of self-control?

Lord, thank You for the reminder that our spiritual journey is a process. Help us to make progress today. In Jesus' name, Amen.

NOTES/INSIGHTS:

FENCING

"Therefore 'If your enemy is hungry, feed him; If he is thirsty, give him a drink; For in so doing you will heap coals of fire on his head.' Do not be overcome by evil, but overcome evil with good."
Romans 12:20-21

At first glance, fencing probably does not seem like an everyday sport, but it has been around since the first modern Olympics, and it has gained popularity in the region where we live. In the past, it was the preparation for sword fighting; in the modern era it has become more associated with swordsmanship and health benefits. Once considered a combat sport, it is now a competitive sport with rules and regulations, and individuals and teams competing all over the world.

The son of a close friend introduced me to Fencing. He competed all through high school, was the best in his class, and he showed me his equipment and gave my family a small demonstration of the moves and objectives.

In fencing, there are two main objectives: the first is to land a point by making contact with the opponent, and second, to ward off attacks from the opponent. Points are landed by making contact with the opponent's gear and setting off a light and sound sensor to let the referee know that contact was made.

A defensive move keeps the opponent's weapon—a Foil, Epee, or Sabre, depending on the weapon—from making contact. In all three forms of fencing, the tip is used to make primary contact, while the blade can only be used in Sabre.

In the Christian life, we are to be making contact with opponents, those who oppose the Gospel of Christ. Along with the mandates of Christian living, Fencing gives us some ideas of how to go about doing that. When facing an opponent, we need to deflect their advances. Instead of getting offended, we need to deflect their antagonism with kindness; we can refuse to be baited into arguments and divisiveness. And, once on offense, we make contact. There is no provision in fencing for an all-out assault on the opponent. Points are made by contact—and points are made by serving our enemies. The passage today says to feed them if they are hungry and to give them a drink when they are thirsty. We make contact at their point of need, and our Heavenly Referee sees those points of contact, and He is pleased with our spiritual sportsmanship. Using our weapons skillfully and carefully, we can break down the defenses of our opponents and work to make contact. We achieve the most when we follow the rules and connect with the ones who oppose us the most.

THOUGHT-PROVOKER:

When was the last time we made good contact with an opponent by following Christ's plan to meet their needs? What do we need to do differently today?

Lord, thank You for showing us how to make contact with an opponent. Help us to use the skills You have given us to make contact at their point of need. In Jesus' name, Amen.

NOTES/INSIGHTS:

Paintball

"But thanks be to God, who gives us the victory through our Lord Jesus Christ. Therefore, my beloved brethren, be steadfast, immovable, always abounding in the work of the Lord, knowing that your labor is not in vain in the Lord."
1 Corinthians 15:57-58

Some good friends and their extended family introduced us to Paintball. We met up at the field—a combination of trees, barrels and man-made barriers—paid attention to the safety guidelines, got the list of rules, picked and loaded our guns, and then chose teams.

There are several different versions of Paintball. There is the "capture the flag" version, where two teams try to capture the flag from the home base of the other team without getting shot. There is the "elimination" version, where everyone plays to shoot the other teams' members, until there is only one player left. And then there is the "no mercy" version, which is where every player keeps playing, regardless of how many times he/she is shot, until there is no ammunition left, or someone gets tired of being pelted and yells, "Mercy!" to leave the game.

Playing Paintball for the first time was great fun. We had on the right clothing and equipment, so while we felt the pellets hit us, no one got terribly hurt, but they did leave bruises. We played several rounds; different versions of capture the flag or elimination, until we got to the last round. The fellows in our group decided to play a final round of No-Mercy, and those pellets, shot at close range and repeatedly, left definite marks on the players.

When we chose to surrender to the gift of salvation provided by Jesus on the cross, we were placed on His team, given our equipment and weapon (Ephesians 6:10-18) and we were placed in the battle. And then, the enemy started pelting us. He keeps coming at us with different versions of the game, hoping to capture our focus, eliminate our testimony or, sometimes, show no mercy as he continues to tear us down and fire at us with everything he has. We, sometimes feel defeated, get bruises on our spirit, and call out for mercy. Paintball has taught us, however, that it's one round. The enemy may come at us for awhile, but Christ has already won the war. At the end of the day, we are the overcomers. The bruises will heal and the battle will be won.

So, today, if you are being pelted by the enemy, if you have bruises, and maybe you want to quit, remember Whose team member you are. Finish the round strong and know the Team Captain knows the outcome, He gives you strength to endure—bruises and all.

THOUGHT-PROVOKER:

What round are you fighting today? What promises do you need to claim to remember you have the victory through Christ?

Lord, thank You for the reminder that You have won the war, especially when we feel like we are being pelted. This is a round, and You give us the victory. Help us to persevere. In Jesus' name, Amen.

NOTES/INSIGHTS:

THE JUMP SHOT

"Therefore humble yourselves under the mighty hand of God, that He may exalt you in due time, casting all your care upon Him, for He cares for you."

1 Peter 5:6-7

I confess that, at five foot, four inches, I am no basketball expert. When I played in Junior High, my best bet was to attempt a half-court shot before the other team realized they could tower over me under the basket. My husband and boys, on the other hand, are all over six feet tall, and they enjoy a good game of pick-up every now and then.

Since I am so short, I watch basketball with a sense of awe. Those tall, lanky bodies moving with grace and resolve down the court. They set up, pass the ball, and then one of them is designated to take the shot. The player sets his/her body toward the basket; everyone's focus turns toward the goal, and then the player lets go. The ball is sent into the air with all the power and precision the player has prepared and when the ball drops into the net, the home crowd cheers.

At five foot, four inches spiritually speaking, I am pretty short too. There have been many great giants of the faith who have prayed better, served more faithfully, and been more of an impact than I can ever hope to be. And yet, we all can stay in the game if we remember two things: we need to keep our focus on the goal—glorifying Christ with our lives and testimonies, and we need to let go. When we focus our attention on the goal, our worries and cares become like that basketball. We stay in the game where God has placed us, and we shoot our cares toward Him. If we hold onto the ball, our team doesn't score. If we hold onto the ball, the other team swarms around us and does their best to take the ball from us to score for themselves. But, when we allow ourselves to focus on the goal and let go of the worries, our team wins. There is an opposing team—the devil wants to spiritually swarm us and make us focus on the ball instead of our goal. There are also witnesses who have gone before us (Hebrews 12) and there are those who are watching us play and encouraging us to score (Ephesians 4). All of them get to celebrate with us when we trust the One who designed the plan of life for us to stay focused on Him, and let go of the ball of cares. Everyone who is routing for us gets to join the celebration when we are obedient and play the game as it was meant to be—letting go of the worry and focusing on the goal.

THOUGHT-PROVOKER

Are we hogging the ball, or are we letting it soar for the basket? Where is our focus?

Lord, please help us to send our worries and cares in Your direction and focus our lives on the goal of glorifying You. Thank you, that when we do that, everyone wins. In Jesus' name, Amen.

NOTES/INSIGHTS:

Snow Skiing

"He is like a man building a house, who dug deep and laid the foundation on the rock. And when the flood arose, the stream beat vehemently against that house, and could not shake it, for it was founded on the rock."

Luke 6:48

I like skiing for the scenery. The beautiful mountains, the crisp white snow, the colorful outfits of skiers zipping down the trails. But, when you have a husband and three kids who love to ski, you take the lessons and you learn to enjoy it with them. No, I am no expert, and I avoid anything that says "Experts" or has a Black Diamond in front of its name, but I do get out on the slopes and make some runs down the intermediate slopes.

One of the key components in skiing is the lean. Every instructor, every decent skier will tell you, as you make your way down the mountain, you must lean into the mountain. This is counterintuitive, because to lean into the mountain, you have to lean uphill. If you lean forward, you will fall, but if you lean back into the mountain, your blades catch correctly and you stay on your feet. The deeper you can lean back into the mountain, the less the wind, and other elements affect you. Your feet stay firmly connected with the blades to the ground and you keep moving.

It's counterintuitive in our lives to lean into the mountain. Our first inclination is to lean down to the see where we are going. That can lead to a nasty tumble. The passage today tells us the builder "dug deep" to lay the foundation in the rock. He had to go against the norm of building on the shore, and he went where the foundation would be sure. He built where his house would stay connected with the ground, even when the elements were beating down on him. The deeper into the rock he went, the more secure his house would be in difficult times. There would be no nasty tumble, because the house would not be shaken.

Lean into your mountain—the security we all have in Jesus Christ. He is eternally the same, His love never changes and His Word is permanent (Hebrews 13). When we struggle in this life to hang on, to avoid the disastrous falls of following our own judgment and following our own ways, we lean into Him. And He keeps us going, with our feet grounded in the truth of His salvation, and moving forward in the hope He has given us. And even when He calls us to the Black Diamond trails of life, we can trust that as long as we lean into Him, He will keep us from falling.

THOUGHT-PROVOKER:

Are we spiritually leaning into the mountain of security we have in Jesus, or are we leaning downhill into our own understanding? What part of our perspective needs to change to make our trip down the trail less treacherous for our spirits?

Lord, thank You that we can lean into You no matter how difficult the trail becomes. Help us to keep leaning into You so that we don't fall. In Jesus' name, Amen.

NOTES/INSIGHTS:

WAKEBOARDING

"Only let your conduct be worthy of the gospel of Christ, so that whether I come and see you or am absent, I may hear of your affairs, that you stand fast in one spirit, with one mind striving together for the faith of the gospel."

Philippians 1:27

Water skiing requires that you be able to sit on your skis as the boat pulls you up out of the water. Wakeboarding, however, tests your ability to stand as you are being pulled up. If you sit on the board, you won't be able to get up to enjoy surfing on the water's surface and be able to jump wakes or do stunts. Because both of your feet are strapped to the same board, you cannot adjust one leg or the other to the pull of the boat—it's an all-in process to stand. My son learned this lesson a few weeks ago as he made the switch from water skiing to wakeboarding. He made several attempts to get up on the board the same way he got up on the skis, and the result was a face full of water and having to restart, because the board would not tilt toward the surface of the water as long as he was leaning back on his legs. When he popped up to a standing position as soon as the boat made tension on the line, he was able to get out of the water and surf the surface. Not only was he able to get up, but he was also able to maneuver the board from side to side and start learning how to do some of the stunts he has seen his friends do on the lake. The key was committing to stand when being put under pressure.

In our spiritual lives, it can be a lot like wakeboarding. We were in the water when God threw us the rescue line of salvation. We cannot do anything in the water without being attached to the boat. Now, as we grow and learn, He allows tension on the rope to pull us up—to get us on the surface of the water so others can see our testimony and realize the dependence we have on Him as the Boat Master. As He allows tension, we have to choose to stand. If we keep holding back, we will continue to get pulled under. If, however, we choose to stand when the pressure is applied, we will get on top of the water, start to enjoy the view and maneuver within the sphere of influence God has given us behind the boat. The pressure is a tool. It keeps us under, or we can choose to stand up against it to get us up where we need to be. The choice is ours. If we want to wakeboard, we have to stand.

THOUGHT-PROVOKER:

Are we standing against the pressure, or letting it pull us under? What does the difference between holding back and standing look like in our lives?

Lord, thank You for the pressure that helps us to get up and stand. Please keep us on our feet this day. In Jesus' name, Amen.

Notes/Insights:

BOWLING

"Jesus said to her, 'I am the resurrection and the life. He who believes in Me, though he may die, he shall live. And whoever lives and believes in Me shall never die. Do you believe this?' She said to Him, 'Yes, Lord, I believe that You are the Christ, the Son of God, who is to come into the world.'"

John 11:25-27

The college-aged young people at our church enjoy bowling, and as the facilitators, we go along for the fun. Most people know the basic rules of bowling—one cannot step over the end line, each player gets two chances to try to wipe out all the pins, gutter balls result in a zero score, etc. What interests me is all the different styles there are for throwing the ball down the alley. One of the girls hurls the ball. It literally does not land on the alley until it is half way, lands with a thud, and then continues on its way. One of the guys spins the ball, using his pinkie and ring finger in two of the holes to control the direction of the ball. Another guy is able to put the ball between his legs, and make an accurate throw. And, my favorite, one young lady, who is new to bowling, throws it granny-style. She puts the ball down and shoves it with both hands towards the pins. No matter the method, each one has the same goal—to hit the pins.

Jesus used different methods with different people, but His goal was always the same: for people to recognize Him as the Messiah, the Only Way to salvation and restoration with the Father. With some, He used quiet conversation, like Nicodemus who came to Him at night (John 3). With others, He used stern warnings; the Pharisees and Sadducees come to mind on several occasions. Still with others, He used parables and miracles to help them understand. In today's passage, He challenged Martha's belief before the miracle came, and she rose to the challenge. She didn't understand all the circumstances, but she knew Who Jesus was and trusted Him.

Churches today are like our college bowlers. Each one may use a different method to share the truth of Jesus Christ. One may use street witnessing or personal evangelism, another may use social media platforms, and still another may use family outreaches into the community. All have the same goal: to introduce others to the saving power of Jesus Christ. And while the methods may differ, the message must be the same: Jesus is The Way, The Truth, and The Life, no one comes to the Father except through Him (John 14:6). As long as we keep the same goal, we can enjoy watching each other's styles and work together to get those pins.

Thought-provoker:

Are we staying true to the message of Jesus Christ? What methods are we using that are working in the areas where we live?

Lord, thank You that You created each of us with a unique personality and creativity. As we use those talents to reach others, please make sure our message stays true to You. In Jesus' name, Amen.

Notes/Insights:

KARATE

"Be anxious for nothing, but in everything by prayer and supplication, with thanksgiving, let your requests be made known to God; and the peace of God, which surpasses all understanding, will guard your hearts and minds through Christ Jesus."

Philippians 4:6-7

"Arms up! You can use your legs to protect your mid-section, but only your arms can protect your face!" I heard this many times in the dojo. I took a sixteen-week self defense course grounded in a form of karate, and our sensei took our personal defense very seriously. He drilled into us that our arms were to be used to protect our faces, senses, and our brains. Karate kicks were fine, and they had their proper place, the mind was defended by the arms.

Drill after drill, we learned how to pull up, push out, and cross our arms to defend from various attacks. Being of small stature, my sensei understood that attackers would go for my head, and I had to be prepared to defend my nose, my cheeks, and other sensitive areas of my head, from attack. His favorite defensive technique for vertically challenged individuals, like me, was to cross our arms in front of our faces, so we still had a line of vision just above where the forearms crossed. It was the "x" that marked the spot of defense in front of the nose, protected the ears and made it possible to drive a blow away from us by thrusting both arms downward at contact and then crossing them right back up again.

Supplication and thanksgiving—the two arms of our spiritual defense. The passage today tells us that we are to use these two defensive strategies. Supplication is telling God about our requests and struggles. Thanksgiving is reminding ourselves that He answers and He promises peace. In karate, a strong opponent may confront us, but knowing the strategies gives us peace that we can stand. Supplication and thanksgiving give us the peace that guards our hearts and minds to be able to stand firm in the spiritual realm. Our heavenly Father knows that peace comes from communication with Him, sharing our concerns and remembering His faithfulness. Being grateful wards off many doubts and knowing He knows what concerns us, and is willing to work what is best for us, fends off fear and worry. So, get your "arms up!" and allow His peace to protect your heart and mind today.

Thought-provoker:

Are we using the defensive strategies God has given us in supplication and thanksgiving, or are we allowing the enemy to attack us with no resistance? What do we need to pray about today?

Dear Lord, thank You for supplication and thanksgiving that allow us to defend ourselves against the attacks of the enemy in spiritual places. Help us to rest in Your peace, knowing You do all things well and for our good. In Jesus' name, Amen.

NOTES/INSIGHTS:

VOLLEYBALL

"And He Himself gave some to be apostles, some prophets, some evangelists, and some pastors and teachers, for the equipping of the saints for the work of ministry, for the edifying of the body of Christ, till we all come to the unity of the faith and of the knowledge of the Son of God, to a perfect man, to the measure of the stature of the fullness of Christ."

Ephesians 4:11-13

W hen I first started teaching several years ago, I was asked to coach the Junior High Volleyball team. I had played volleyball in intramurals in college, but I had to learn the strategies and techniques in order to be able to coach.

What I learned was each member on the court, regardless of where they start in the floor rotation at service, has a job to do. There are those who are good at serving the ball from the back line, there are those who set the ball up, and then there are those who attack the ball after it is set. On the defensive side, there are those who dig the ball back up after a deep serve, those who can block at the net and those who react quickly to ball placement by the opposing team and keep the ball in play. As each team member plays the correct position, the team unifies and works toward winning a set. Communication and strategy are key components, but so is playing one's position. A good coach figures out which players have certain skill sets, and a great coach develops those skill sets and motivates a team to work off each other's strengths.

God has given each of us spiritual gifts that are meant to serve the team. Some are good at serving—prayer warriors who place the ball in play by holding others up and going after the opposing team in the spiritual realms. Others are able to set the ball—leaders and teachers who are able to explain the Word so others can take it in and then go on the attack. The attackers—those evangelists and workers who go after the lost and entreat them to come to the Savior. Just as important, the defensive players who are willing to dig deep and keep the ball in play, either through financial means or faithfulness in their home churches. The blockers—those who keep fighting on the front lines of faith and not allowing the enemy to bring harm to the family of God, and then those who act—those who give all to go into full-time ministry and move wherever God calls them to, so the ball stays in play in the far reaches of the world. If you know your position, get in the game. If you are not sure, ask God to reveal your place and be grateful to be a part of His team. Together, we are unstoppable—even the gates of Hell will not prevail against us.

THOUGHT-PROVOKER:

What position has God gifted you to play on His team? Are you where you should be?

Dear Lord, thank You for Your perfect design and Your good gifts You have given. Help each of us to play the position You have called us to and please allow us to win victories for Your glory. In Jesus' name, Amen.

NOTES/INSIGHTS:

TENNIS

"He who does not love does not know God, for God is love. In this the love of God was manifested toward us, that God has sent His only begotten Son into the world, that we might live through Him. In this is love, not that we loved God, but that He loved us and sent His Son to be the propitiation for our sins."

1 John 4:8-10

I grew up learning to play tennis. My dad played with several people from work, and my mom joined in for doubles. My sister and I were not old enough to stay home alone, so we found ourselves at the tennis court. Instead of sitting on the bleachers bored, and possibly getting into trouble, my sister and I played as well. Our parents got each of us a racket and started to teach us the game. We were given a bottle of tennis balls, shown the boundaries, told the basic rules, and we would play on a court a short distance away from where the adults were practicing. Sometimes, a couple of the adults would walk over and challenge us to a friendly game, or give us some pointers on how to improve our serve or our swings.

For some reason, the backhand swing was a challenge for

me. It was awkward, but I kept working at it. It paid off too, because my first date with my husband was on the tennis court, and while I was no where near his athletic ability, he thought I was cute, we were married less than a year later, and that was over twenty-five years ago now. Guess it was love on the court.

Love. The word used in tennis for scoring. Before we serve a single point, before we hit a single ball, we are hit with love. "Love, all." "Love, fifteen." "Thirty, love." We hear these phrases, and we wonder why "love" would be the call for someone who has done nothing to earn points, to win the set, or to win the overall match. I think it is a perfect word to describe the score of life. Before we've done a single thing, love. Before we can try to make a mark on the world, or make a difference on the court, love. God's love. Every new set, love. Every time we start again, love. Every time we've been defeated, and we play again, love. Every time we win, we start back at love. He loves us from before the beginning of time, and He will love us to eternity. So, if we have failed, trust His love. If we have won, trust His love. The score tells it all. His love never fails.

THOUGHT-PROVOKER:

How does knowing the love of God never fails motivate us as His children today? Are you willing to risk stepping onto the court, knowing the score always starts with love?

Dear Father, thank You for Your love and that it is always our starting point, and has nothing to do with how we win or lose today. Help us to walk onto the court confident in Your love today for Your glory. In Jesus' name, Amen.

NOTES/INSIGHTS:

THE OFFENSIVE LINE

*"And we urge you, brethren, to recognize those who labor
among you, and are over you in the Lord and admonish you,
and to esteem them very highly in love for their work's sake.
Be at peace among yourselves."*

1 Thessalonians 5:12-13

Football has an interesting concept—it is called an offensive
line, but its job is full-time defense. The offensive line's job is to
protect the quarterback so that he can complete a pass or a hand-
off to make progress down the field. Without the offensive line,
the quarterback is vulnerable to pressure and takedowns from
the opposing team's defense. He cannot focus on his primary job
because he is concerned for his safety as huge defensive backs
head his way and plan to stop him from completing the plays.

But, with a strong offensive line, the quarterback is able to
concentrate on seeing the field of players, find the open player
and to complete plays as his team marches down the field. With
the offensive line in place, the quarterback can do what he is
called to do, and with a spiritual offensive line in place, a pastor
can do what he is called to do. So, what are a spiritual offensive
line's responsibilities? According to 1 Thessalonians, we are to
recognize those who labor among us. To recognize them means
to identify with them and give them validation. It means we

are not willing to listen to unsound gossip about our leaders and we refuse to participate in any conversations that put them down. Instead, we hold our pastors and leaders in high esteem. We love them, and we are at peace among ourselves so they are not distracted by us. In other places in Scripture, we learn that we are to pray for them (1 Timothy 2), submit to them (1 Peter 5) and honor them (1 Timothy 5). By doing these things, we build a line of defense that helps to protect our leaders and their families from the attacks of the enemy.

Without the line being held, the quarterback becomes vulnerable, and without a quarterback, the line has no purpose on the field. When both work together, the team moves forward, the opposing team is pushed back, and points are scored. In the spiritual realm, when we hold our leaders up in prayer and reverence, the kingdom moves forward, the enemy is pushed back, and lives are changed for eternity. These are good things for which we all should strive, and if we find ourselves on that offensive line, we need to fall to our knees, take our stance, and get ready for battle. Protect those who serve us by praying, submitting, honoring, loving and recognizing them. This is how we move our churches forward.

THOUGHT-PROVOKER:

Have we prayed for our leaders today? Are we holding the line of honor and submission so we can all move forward? Are we at peace to keep from being a distraction to them?

Dear Father, thank You for our pastors and leaders who honor You by serving us. Help us to recognize, esteem, and honor them and to be sure we pray for them and submit to them as You have designed so Your church can move forward. In Jesus' name, Amen.

NOTES/INSIGHTS:

THE INJURY

"For where envy and self-seeking exist, confusion and every evil thing are there. But the wisdom that is from above is first pure, then peaceable, gentle, willing to yield, full of mercy and good fruits, without partiality and without hypocrisy. Now the fruit of righteousness is sown in peace by those who make peace."

James 3:16-18

Just when the workout routine has started to work, when the team has turned the corner and the wins are coming faster than the losses, or when that personal record is within reach—it happens. Something in the body breaks down, the wrong type of contact is made on the field, or someone lands awkwardly, and an injury occurs. A broken clavicle for a quarterback, a broken ankle for a forward, or a concussion and what was a promising season gets sidelined.

No one likes injuries. No one goes out and says, "I think I'd like to be injured today" or "I hope I hurt something today so I have to sit out for six to eight weeks." And, sometimes, our injuries are not our fault. But, sometimes, they are. Sometimes, we don't listen to our bodies' signals about a breakdown, or we don't listen to a coach's instruction about how to land or how to fall. We think we've got it. We think we can handle a particular element on our own. We get in our own way of progress.

Words are a lot like those injuries. They weren't intended to be said and cause pain. No one says, "I think I will damage a relationship today" or "Let's see how much hurt I can cause my parents, my spouse, or my friend." But, sometimes, we do. We don't listen to the cautions of Scripture, we give into our selfishness or anger, and we spew something that we cannot take back. The relationship that was going so well—silenced by hurt and disappointment. The team mentality of the family moving in a positive direction—takes a nose dive when the pain of hurtful words cuts off communication. And our progress is sidelined.

In most cases, physical injuries heal. Doctors apply medical wisdom, we are humbled to follow instructions, and healing brings us back. It takes time, and we must be willing to work through it, rest, and let the broken pieces be restored. If we allow, emotional injuries can heal as well, but we have to yield to the Scripture's wisdom of humility, forgiveness and restoration. Today's passage reminds us that progress is made in the paths of humility, purity, and gentleness. Peace comes through the healing process of righteousness and restoration. May we be agents of healing today.

THOUGHT-PROVOKER:

What injuries have we caused by selfish choice of words? What are we doing to bring about restoration to those injuries?

Lord, thank You that You are the Great Physician and that healing is part of Your great love for us. Help us to be careful not to cause injury through our words, and when we do, help us to repent, and restore those relationships. In Jesus' name, Amen.

NOTES/INSIGHTS:

RUNNING

"Then Jesse said to his son David, "Take now for your brothers an ephah of this dried grain and these ten loaves, and run to your brothers at the camp."

1 Samuel 17:17

Running is one of those love-hate relationships—an athlete either loves it, or sees it as a punishment. I have heard many of the sayings and the jokes too—"My sport is your sports punishment," and even "The Bible says not to run unless someone pursues, so who is chasing you?" Running helps to condition the body and prepare endurance. It also helps to relieve stress and release endorphins. It produces cardiac fitness and burns fat. Yet, none of these factors mattered to Jesse.

Jesse wanted David to get to the frontlines and supply his brothers with food, and then he wanted David to get back to him with news from the front. He wanted David to focus, stay on task, and not get distracted, so he told him to run. David wasn't supposed to poke along, or stop when he felt like it; he was to get where he was going and do the job he was sent to do.

Running put David right where he needed to be to see the threat of Goliath. If he would have walked or meandered, he would have missed Goliath's challenge. By running, David made it in time for the battle. David ran to the battle, not away from it. We don't get better at running by taking breaks and sitting on greenways. We get better by running. God was preparing David for a battle he didn't even know he was going to fight. Physical running can prepare us for races, and for times when we need added strength. Spiritually, running—working harder at our spiritual disciplines and being intentional about holy living—prepares us for an unseen future.

Sometimes, in our lives, we must be ready to run toward the calling God has for us in that moment. When He has given clear direction, when His commandments are vivid and direct, when our passion for Him overrides our excuses, we need to run toward what He has for us. If we do not, we will miss the moment—we will miss the challenge, and others will run away from the battle in their fear (17:24). Because of David's trust in God, he was able to run toward the giant, and he brought about a great victory that enabled others to run also (17:49). Because David took up his challenge, the army took up theirs, pursued the enemy and was able to overcome (17:52). So, the next time we find ourselves running, know that God is preparing us for what is to come, and run toward it.

Thought-provoker:

What direction are we running today—toward or away from the battle? What needs to change?

Lord, thank You for David's courage to run toward the battle, even when he didn't know what he was preparing for, and his trust in You that enabled him to run toward it. Help us do the same and win victories in Your name. In Jesus' name, Amen.

Running

NOTES/INSIGHTS:

THE BENCH

"And the things that you have heard from me among many witnesses, commit these to faithful men who will be able to teach others also."

2 Timothy 2:2

Bench time. Part of being on a team is sitting on the bench. Not every player can be on the field or court at the same time. In some sports, the defense gets a break while the offense works to score; in other sports, players take turns sitting out to give one another a break and to put fresh energy in the game. On occasion, I have heard players say that they hate to sit the bench; they would rather be in the game.

Most of these players seem to think they have endless energy and are able to see all the aspects of the game while they are playing, but a wise coach knows better. A wise coach knows some bench time allows the players to see what is happening at both ends of the court or field, and it also gives them a chance to hear what he is saying without having to yell. The coach also understands that bench time is also an opportunity to rehydrate, refocus and get ready to get back into the game with a greater sense of urgency and intensity because the athletes have a had a few minutes to rest their muscles and catch their breath.

Bench time is not a waste of time, especially in the spiritual game. There were times that even Jesus sat the bench for a bit. If that seems outrageous, check out Matthew 14, John 6. These passages recount the time that Jesus went up into a mountain alone after being very busy in ministry. He took the time to pray and be alone with the Father. He didn't stay out long—He was back walking on the water in the next few verses and challenging the disciples to walk by faith, but He took time to sit the bench. And there are times when He asks us to sit the bench, take a break, and get reenergized for the game. Paul tells Timothy to choose faithful men to teach, so they can get back in the game and teach others also. Faithful—players who are already involved and committed in the team mission. They just need some time to learn more and to be able to then pass it on to others. So, when we need bench time, take it. Don't stay out of the game for long, but use that time to rehydrate, refocus, learn and get ready to jump back in. Bench time—it's a good thing.

Thought-provoker:

How do we view bench time? Are we taking the time we are asked to take a break from the game to learn, to refresh and reenergize? What bench time do we need today?

Dear Lord, thank You for bench time. Please help us to take the time we need to learn, to rest, and to refocus so we can play our best for You. In Jesus' name, Amen.

Notes/Insights:

FISHING

"Be still, and know that I am God; I will be exalted among the nations, I will be exalted in the earth!"

Psalm 46:10

When I was a child, my dad would take me to a small lake for some catch and release fishing, not too far from our house. We would sometimes walk to it with our fishing gear. I say, gear, because he would take his pole, tackle box, and bait, I would take a baggie full of bread. Once we got to the lake, my dad would get all set up—put bait on the hooks, find a good spot to cast, and he would fish. I would get bored. Being quiet, and sitting or standing still, when there was so much to see and do at the edge of the lake, was tough for a kid. And I had my bag of bread. It wouldn't be too long, and I would be at the water's edge, checking out tadpoles, and trying to catch a few. I would disturb the waters, the fish would scatter, and my dad would graciously say, "Stay here. I am going to move down a little ways to fish." I would gladly comply, and he would move further down the shore.

After I saw he was settled in and fishing again, I would plop down on the bank and open my bag of bread. I would break off small pieces and throw them on the water. It wouldn't be long, and the fish would return. They nibbled at the bread, and I got to have "conversations" with the fish, because I was being still, and I had offered them a treat. Eventually, I would have so many fish snacking on my bread treats that my dad would come back closer to where I was and he would catch a few fish on the outer circle of the breadcrumbs.

I know this is not the type of fishing most people think of when they think of sport fishing. There are many competitive fishing tournaments and serious lake fishers, but these memories of fishing made a connection for me in my spiritual life recently. I realized as I was reading through the New Testament that not one time did Jesus shout someone into a salvation decision. Most of the time, He sat and conversed with them, and offered them the Bread of Life in one form or another. It may have been in a large arena—the days He taught, and fed, thousands come to mind. Or, it may have been a one-on-one conversation with a Centurion or a Sadducee. The connection for me was this—go to where the fish are, be calm, and offer them the bread. In our world, we don't need more yelling; we need more telling. Tell them about Jesus.

THOUGHT-PROVOKER:

Are we offering the Bread of Life to the unbelievers around us? How are we offering it?

Lord, thank You for the reminder to be still and that salvation comes when we share the Bread of Life with those around us. Help us to remember to tell it, not yell it. In Jesus' name, Amen.

NOTES/INSIGHTS:

CHEERLEADING

"And let us consider one another in order to stir up love and good works, not forsaking the assembling of ourselves together, as is the manner of some, but exhorting one another, and so much the more as you see the Day approaching."

Hebrews 10:24-25

Cheerleaders have a tough job. No, not the cheerleaders whose team is winning 38-0 and it is the last five minutes of the game. Their job is to keep smiling, congratulating the winners, and keeping the crowd enthusiastic about the imminent win. Those cheerleaders have the momentum and the crowd's energy on their side. The winning cheerleaders can easily encourage others—their team, the crowd, each other—to smile and enjoy the win.

The tough-job cheerleaders are those who have to keep cheering when their team is the zero in that score. When things are not going their way, and when the crowd has all but packed up and gone home, these cheerleaders are expected to stay out on the edge of that field and keep on encouraging. Exhorting, is actually the word used in Hebrews, and its meaning includes the concept of consolation. Consolation, as in the prize you win for not winning. It's the idea of we'll try again next time, or keep your heads up, this is only one game. The cheerleaders in this type of situation have a much more difficult task. There is no momentum on their side, the crowd is not cheering, and yet, they do. They keep cheering.

Cheerleaders are there for two reasons: leading, and cheering. According to Hebrews, Christians are cheerleaders. Today's passage says to stir up love and good works—this is the cheering we all like to do. When the kingdom is advancing, when the Lord is visibly working and we see the results, it is easier to encourage one another to keep on going, to do better, to push forward. But, the passage goes on to say, that we are to keep showing up (not forsaking the assembly), and exhorting one another—there's that consolation concept—even in difficult times. When we don't have visible proof that our side is advancing, when we are discouraged, when others are packing up and leaving, we stay and cheer. Not because our coach demands it, but because we need it. We need to be reminded that it's just one battle—our Commander has already won the war. We need to be reminded that we can keep our heads up as the children of God, and that we will be here, on this same field, game after game, cheering. Cheering, regardless of the temporary score, regardless of where the momentum shifts, no matter who the opponent is, we cheer. And when we do, God hears it, and it makes Him proud.

Thought-provoker:

Are we leading the cheering where we are? Are we encouraging those who are seeing victories? Are we exhorting those who are in difficult times?

Dear Lord, thank You that we can cheer, no matter what the present game looks like, because we know You have already won the championship. Help us to help others. In Jesus' name, Amen.

NOTES/INSIGHTS:

GYMNASTICS

*"But I discipline my body and bring it into subjection, lest, when
I have preached to others, I myself should become disqualified."*
1 Corinthians 9:27

There are a few young ladies at our church who participate in gymnastics. They go to the gym several times a week, and when we have free time at church, we can watch as they show each other the latest moves they have learned. They can run, flip, twist, turn and bend in ways that just do not seem possible. They practice hard, learn routines, and go to competitions.

I have sat and talked with a few of them about the gymnastics, and one of the recurring themes is self-control. They have to learn how many steps they can take, and which moves they can do within a certain space, because if they cross a line, they are disqualified. They have to bend their bodies and control their movements so they stay within the boundaries of the gymnastics floor on which they compete. They can have a flawless routine as far as the moves, but if they step over a boundary, it doesn't matter. The judges, those who are watching and scrutinizing their routines, disqualify them and the routines no longer matter.

In today's culture, it seems a lot of lines have been blurred.

So, how do Christians navigate? What routines, gymnastically speaking, are okay to do, and where are the boundary lines? Paul, the writer of the passage today, also says in Titus: "in all things showing yourself to be a pattern of good works; in doctrine showing integrity, reverence, incorruptibility, sound speech that cannot be condemned, that one who is an opponent may be ashamed, having nothing evil to say of you," (2:7-8). Paul breaks it down into parts we can apply to our daily routines: a pattern of good works—making sure our outward behavior is fitting for the Kingdom of God. Integrity in our doctrine—making sure we teach true to the Word of God. Reverence—showing respect for the things of God and toward those who deserve to be held in honor. Incorruptibility—not being taken in by the deception of power, riches or evil influences, and sound speech—making sure what comes out of our mouths is good, true and encouraging. All of this adds up to a life that shames our opponent and gives him nothing evil to say about us. So, today, let's stay within the boundaries of the spiritual realm by bending our flesh to the routines that lead to a qualifying reward, instead of stepping over lines and being disqualified in the eyes of those who are watching, and scrutinizing, our walk.

THOUGHT-PROVOKER:

What boundaries do we need in our lives so those around us will see we are different in Christ?

Lord, thank You for the Holy Spirit's leading, and Your Word, that help us to stay within the boundaries and have a life that others can see You in and through. Help us to stay qualified today by bending our flesh to Your routines. In Jesus' name, Amen.

Notes/Insights:

WATER SKIING

"For this is the will of God, your sanctification: that you should abstain from sexual immorality; that each of you should know how to possess his own vessel in sanctification and honor, not in passion of lust, like the Gentiles who do not know God."
1 Thessalonians 4:3-5

Our family enjoys water sports. From swimming to skiing, we have fun on the lake. Something about being outside, seeing the beauty of nature, and getting some exercise with the bonus of the water to keep us from sweating, it's a good fit. We also enjoy taking friends out to the lake and teaching them how to enjoy water sports too.

The first step is to stay behind the boat. Sounds simple enough, but many times new skiers think they need to get up and head out to the side of the wake. While the wake is intimidating, it actually smooths the water out right behind the boat and makes a great place to learn the footing to ski. Even experienced skiers who ride or jump the wake still have to stay behind the boat—it's physically impossible for the skier to be in front of the boat.

The second step is to trust the driver. If the skier is worried about where the driver is going, he or she won't stay focused on putting tension on the skis and gradually coming up out of the water. The driver knows how much power it will take to get the skier up, where the dangers are on the lake, and how to stay clear of them. The skier's job is to put resistance on the skis and allow the boat to do the pull work.

Third, the skier has to relax. Getting up tight about the process makes muscles tense and rising out of the water difficult. The skier has to trust the process and know that skiing works when one follows the instructions.

God has set out a specific way for His children to live—and He is the Master Teacher. He knows the big picture of life needs to be broken into manageable instructions that can be followed. Our job is to stay in the wake of the instructions He created for us, and to trust that He knows where the boat is going. When He says, "Abstain from sexual immorality," it is not because He is trying to keep something from us, it is because He knows that following the world's waves will never fill our desires for intimacy and a true love relationship. The world offers failure and misery; He offers deep love and security in a relationship built within a marriage as He designed. And, we need to relax. When the Master designs a plan, He will make sure it works. Stay in His wake today.

THOUGHT-PROVOKER:

Are we staying in the wake of God's loving instructions? If we aren't, what steps are we going to take to restore our relationship with Him today?

Dear Lord, thank You for the instructions that are clear in Your Word so we know where our boundaries need to be. Help us to relax in Your love and trust in Your guidance today. In Jesus' name, Amen.

NOTES/INSIGHTS:

THE STARTING LINE

"You ran well. Who hindered you from obeying the truth?"
Galatians 5:7

Every race, match, game or friendly backyard competition starts somewhere. There is a line designated where everyone lines up to start awaiting a pistol shot, a timer, or the whistle blow to indicate time for the teams to be on the field. There isn't a game, match or race without a start. And each new opportunity to compete brings a new starting line.

Runners have a great visual of this concept. At every race, there is a big sign or a line painted on the ground that indicates the beginning of the race. And it doesn't matter if it's your very first race, or you are a veteran of the sport, that line means you have to face the clock and get ready to go. Everyone lines up, everyone packs in, and everyone takes off at the sound of the starting gun. If you aren't careful, you can get tripped up right at the start. Someone with a different pace runs too slowly in front of you, or someone who is faster than you gets too close and you trip as they run right by. Each runner is running to compete, but each runner has to run at his or her own pace.

There was a big race in the city close to where we live and I had trained for months to be ready. We lined up in our different chutes and as the gun went off, someone from behind came flying past me, and he inadvertently tripped me at the starting gate. As I fell, my heart filled with disappointment as I missed my first goal of the race, to start strong.

Today's passage asks the question, "Who hindered you from obeying the truth?" Who tripped you up? What stopped you from getting that strong start you were hoping for as you tried to go deeper in your spiritual journey? Who, or what, is stopping you now? When, because it happens to all of us, we find ourselves sitting on the curb, wondering how we fell from grace, missed our expectations, or allowed someone else to hinder our progress, we need to take a deep, spiritual breath. The race is not over. We have permission to get back in the line up and get going in the race direction again.

And that day, that is what I did. I got up, and I got going again. Another runner offered me a hand up, I set my pace, and I got back in the race. So, today, whether you are lining up at the start for the first time, or the millionth time, stay in the race. Keep your pace. The race is not over until we see the finish line at the heavenly gate. Until then, start again.

Thought-provoker:

Where are we in the spiritual run of our lives today? What hindrance do we need to drop so we can line up for a fresh start today?

Dear Lord, thank You for new starts. Help us to keep on running until we see You. In Jesus' name, Amen.

Notes/Insights:

SURFCASTING

"For we do not have a High Priest who cannot sympathize with our weaknesses, but was in all points tempted as we are, yet without sin. Let us therefore come boldly to the throne of grace, that we may obtain mercy and find grace to help in time of need."

Hebrews 4:15-16

Surfcasting, also known as beach casting, is fishing from the shoreline of a beach along, or just beyond, the surf. There are two types of surfcasting—hand held, in which the fisherman, or woman, casts the line and then holds the rod and reel, and then there is the stand-held, where the fisher casts the line and then places the pole in a stand and waits for the reel to spin. The reel is out of the hand of the fisher; he/she simply waits on a fish to grab the line.

Praying is a lot like surfcasting. We are supposed to cast our cares on the Lord (1 Peter 5:7), and then we wait. It doesn't do any good for us to become anxious about the answer—the fish takes the bait when the timing is right; answers come when they are in God's perfect timing. We can pace up and down the beach, we can call someone and fret about the surf, the wind, or the heat, or we can do what the elderly gentlemen outside our hotel room this past summer did—sit down and enjoy the wait. Yes, two gentlemen were surfcasting outside our hotel, and each morning they set their lines, pushed their long poles into the stands, and then the two men sat and waited. They chatted and they waited. They didn't pace the beach, and they didn't keep checking their lines. They knew that the reels would let them know when the fish were on the line. Each morning, they followed the same routine. And each day, they caught fish. Sometimes the fish were little, and once in awhile, they caught some really big ones.

God knows that we anticipate answers. He also knows that many answers to our prayers are out of our control—we cannot reel them in by fretting on the shoreline. God knows we learn patience and endurance in times of waiting, and they are just as important as any answers He will send. And He does send answers. He understands us and He knows the best timing for us to catch some answers. He has walked the shoreline, and He knows the answers we seek. He wants us to sit and wait, and because He loves us, He will send the answers. We can cast the line of prayer, knowing our High Priest is ready, and willing, to answer at just the right moment.

Thought-provoker:

Are we anxious about casting our prayers? How do we wait as the answers come?

Lord, thank You that You control the timing of our answers and You help us as we wait. Thank You that You care, and that You do send answers. In Jesus' name, Amen.

NOTES/INSIGHTS:

Hunter Jumping

"Having then gifts differing according to the grace that is given to us, let us use them: if prophecy, let us prophesy in proportion to our faith; or ministry, let us use it in our ministering; he who teaches, in teaching; he who exhorts, in exhortation; he who gives, with liberality; he who leads, with diligence; he who shows mercy, with cheerfulness."

Romans 12:6-8

We have a friend who rides horses that jump fences. She has one horse that can clear a fence that is as tall as I am, and although I am five foot four and considered humanly short, it still impresses me that her horse could literally jump over me if he wished. She has trained this horse to hop on a trailer, travel to a show, stay in a strange barn with lots of different horses, get ready and compete. He does all of this well, and he wins a lot of ribbons. He was made to be a hunter jumper horse.

What her horse cannot do, however, is go out on trail rides. He is so used to working in an arena, having his immense strength bounded by rails and channeled by his rider's cues, that when he is released from that arena to go ride trails in the woods, he freaks out. Literally, his body shakes and he refuses to go. He snorts, picks his front feet off the ground and does his best to get back to the arena, or the barn next to it. This horse knows that he was not called to go slowly through the woods and enjoy the view. He is the type of horse that has energy, strength and assertiveness in the arena, but he is very unsure of himself anywhere else.

We should all be like this horse in one specific way. We should figure out what we have been called to do, submit to the Lord's leading and training, and stick to it. God has not called all of us to do the same things, or to do everything ourselves. And,—let's be honest here—when we try to do too much, or what we are not called to do, we get a little freaked out. When we stay within the bounds of what He has prepared us to do in His kingdom, we excel. We learn to trust Him deeply and we find the peace and joy of being right where He wants us. According to our passage today, we have gifts that were given in grace, and we should use them. We get more done for His glory when we each live in our callings.

THOUGHT-PROVOKER:

What is each of our different callings, and how are we living those out in our lives? Are there some things we should not do, or give up? What does a called life look like?

Lord, thank You that You did not call us all to the same things. Help each of us to do what You have called us to do, and be a blessing to those around us in those ways. In Jesus' name, Amen.

NOTES/INSIGHTS:

PICKLE BALL

"For I am not ashamed of the gospel of Christ, for it is the power of God to salvation for everyone who believes, for the Jew first and also for the Greek. For in it the righteousness of God is revealed from faith to faith; as it is written, 'The just shall live by faith.'"

Romans 1:16-17

Pickle Ball is a unique sport. This is probably an oversimplified definition, but it's ping-pong on a tennis or badminton court. The rules are basically the same, it is played with wooden paddles and a whiffle ball, and nearly anyone can play. Children, grandparents, teenagers, middle-agers, athletes, handicapped—everyone can play. The easiest way to learn is to be invited to play with others who know the game. They guide a new player through the rules and help them enjoy as they play. Almost everyone I know who plays the game is patient, kind, ready, and willing to share his or her joy of it with others. The game itself is easy to learn, and easy to pass along to others.

Pickle Ball reminds me of the Gospel. The Gospel is simple to understand—the Scriptures say even a child can accept it (Matthew 18). In Pickle Ball, children are encouraged to come on the court and play with other players. According to the Pickle Ball Association, the game was started with children in mind. Another parallel is that all are welcome (Romans 10). No matter the age, status or athleticism, everyone is welcome to come and learn the game. God does not put a stipulation on the age, status or education of someone to come into the kingdom. In fact, the Scriptures are full of young and old, rich and poor, layman and skilled, who all hear the Word of God and respond in faith, and He receives them (John 1:12).

The players are like believers—it's our job to show others the plan of salvation and allow them to join us on the court to hear the word of faith and receive it (Matthew 28:18-20). The Pickle Ball players I know are proud of the game they play, and they are excited to share it with those who are interested. They give them time to learn the game, to understand what they are doing, and to decide for themselves to become players. With the Gospel, we do the same. We are not ashamed of it, we share it, and we give others the opportunity to accept it for themselves. Today, we should be the players who share the Gospel, and pray that God brings new players onto the team.

Thought-provoker:

Are we ashamed to share the Gospel, or do we encourage others to come and learn? How can we do a better job of sharing the Gospel like Pickle Ball players share their sport?

Lord, help us to share the great news of the Gospel like Pickle Ball players share their game with others. Help us to reveal our joy and invite others to join in. In Jesus' name, Amen.

NOTES/INSIGHTS:

SKATING

"Surely goodness and mercy shall follow me all the days of my life; and I will dwell in the house of the Lord forever."
Psalm 23:6

There are all kinds of different skates. Ice skates, roller-skates, and roller blades are all part of the skate family. There are many different sports played on skates as well. Hockey, figure skating, speed skating, roller derby, inline skating and artistic skating are some of the sports that come to mind. In each of these sports, the skater has to learn balance. Each skater learns techniques to stop, turn, go backwards and even jump while keeping their blades in balance. Roller skaters learn to weave their wheels in between obstacles for artistic skating, and how to get low and fast for speed racing. Figure skaters learn to put their main focus on the middle of the blade as they push gracefully across the ice, while hockey players push on the outside of the blades to gain speed as they target the puck. Each skater has to learn to shift his/her weight from one leg to the other to propel their momentum forward, and to keep their balance as they move across the ice.

Goodness and mercy are the blades of balance in life. The goodness of God, balanced with the mercy of God, keeps us from falling as we skate on life's ice. God's goodness, His grace toward us to give us blessings, in spite of our shortcomings, helps us to stay balanced on the straight-a-ways—the times we are grateful for as they are full of joy and good memories. But, sometimes the weight shifts, and we need the blade of mercy. The times God does not give us what we deserve because of what we have done, but He shows love and forgiveness as we traverse the dark times on the ice. When the spotlights have gone out, and we live in the darkness of our hidden sin, He brings us back into the light of forgiveness and gets us back in His will for our lives.

We need both to be able to stand. Without God's goodness, we become discouraged and life becomes meaningless. The author of Ecclesiastes investigated all kinds of pleasures in life, and he came to call them all "vanity" without the reverence for God and His goodness in his life. Without God's mercy, we see our constant failures and our wretchedness in our sin. The tax collector in Luke 18:14 beat his breast, saying, "God, be merciful to me a sinner!" He knew God's mercy was his only chance to have any opportunity to be justified. Having both means we can stay balanced, as we are grateful that He is both good, and merciful, to us. We need both skates to be able to stand on the ice.

THOUGHT-PROVOKER:

Are we grateful for both God's goodness and mercy, or do we take both for granted? How should we live differently in the light of both in our lives?

Lord, thank You for both Your grace and mercy. Help us to stay balanced in our lives by thanking You for both, and taking neither one for granted. In Jesus' name, Amen.

Notes/Insights:

HIKING

"Show me Your ways, O Lord; teach me Your paths. Lead me in Your truth and teach me, for You are the God of my salvation; on You I wait all the day."

Psalm 25:4-5

There are some beautiful hiking trails not far from our home. A national park, with lots of history and interesting natural landscapes, is a great place to take friends and family when they come to visit. There are long trails with hilly challenges for the athletically inclined, and there are shorter, easier trails for those who just want some recreation and fresh air.

The important thing to know is which trail is which. If we are out for some recreation, we want to be on the green trails—shorter, level trails that make for a good walk while talking about the day, or catching up with old friends. It's not a good idea to take the blue trails if we just want to walk and talk. The blue trails have hilly challenges and longer passes through the woods. If we want to talk on blue trails, we might have to stop and catch our breath along the way. And then there are the cable trails—trails that have cables strapped into the rock that we have to hold onto to pull ourselves up, or to keep ourselves from going down too fast. Those trails require concentration and attention to each step. There is very little conversation when we are traversing those as we each have to focus on our steps and our hand holds as we go.

God knows each trail; He is the expert Trail Guide. He knows each of the different seasons of life as we pass through them, and He knows whether we need to be on an easy trail where we can converse easily with Him as we walk on, or if we need something steeper to test our character and help us to trust Him deeper as we change elevations. He knows the best path for each of us as we hike life's terrain. He knows when we need to stop and rest, and when He needs to push us. I am thankful for different trails. Life would be tedious if we were always cable climbing, and it would be boring if trails were always level and easy. God, in His wisdom, leads us to the right path for each season. We need to trust His guidance and accept the terrain. Even when we feel challenged, it is then that we can grow.

THOUGHT-PROVOKER:

Which trail do we find ourselves on in this season of life? Are we trusting God knows where we are and why we are here, or are we pushing back on the path He has for us? What steps do we need to take today?

Dear Father, thank You for different trails for different seasons of life. Help us to trust You as You lead us, and help us to take the next step on the trail so we keep moving forward. In Jesus' name, Amen.

Notes/Insights:

THE BACKWARDS "K"

"If then you were raised with Christ, seek those things which
are above, where Christ is, sitting at the right hand of God.
Set your mind on things above, not on things on the earth."
Colossians 3:1-2

In baseball, there is a book where every move a player makes is recorded. It's recorded in dashes, lines, and letters. It tells every strike, ball and hit they have in the game. It tells who made the play, who assisted with the out, and how many pitches were thrown. And the one statistic every baseball player tries to avoid is the backwards "K."

In the book, a "K" means the player struck out at the plate. A backwards "K" means the player struck out at the plate without even swinging. The player was standing at the plate, ready to engage and run the bases. He is given at least three opportunities to hit the ball, and on the last count—whether it was two strikes and no balls, or a full count—he stood there. His body was present in the game, but he didn't set his eyes on the ball, and he missed it.

Scripture admonishes us to set our eyes on things above—to get focused on the things that matter to God in the game of life. He wants us engaged in the ministry (2 Timothy 2) and He wants us to let other distractions go (I John 2). He wants us to love others, encourage others, put the ball of compassion into play, and we find ourselves standing there. We see the need, we know the play needs to be made, but we don't swing. God has us standing at the plate. He wants us to stop worrying (Phil 4) and put the ball in play. It doesn't matter to Him if we simply take a meal across the street or we fill a tractor-trailer with boxes of food for an entire community. It takes all types of plays to make the win in baseball. God can use us to lift someone's spirits as we smile at them on the morning commute, and allow them to merge in busy morning traffic. He can use us to speak the good news of the Gospel over a cup of coffee with a friend. And yes, we are sometimes blessed to have the home run hit of our lives when we take a big step of faith and He allows us to see souls brought into the fold in a big way. What hurts His heart is when we take the backwards "K." When we get distracted with ourselves, and we don't meet the needs. So, today, see the need and make the play. Our team doesn't need to take anymore backwards "K's."

THOUGHT-PROVOKER:

Where do we tend to see a need and not meet it? What do we need to change in our focus so we are in tune with what God wants done?

Lord, thank You that You accept us as we are and still allow us to meet needs in Your kingdom. Help us to make the play today when we see the needs You want us to meet. In Jesus' name, Amen.

NOTES/INSIGHTS:

Dodge Ball

"But You, O Lord, are a shield for me, my glory and the One who lifts up my head. I cried to the Lord with my voice, and He heard me from His holy hill. Selah."

Psalm 3:3-4

You either love it, or hate it. Dodge Ball. Just the sound of it either makes us excited or anxious. We've played this game since we were in grade school. It seemed to be the gym teacher's favorite on Fridays when I was growing up. We'd line up in the gym, pick teams and head onto the court. The balls started flying, and we were dodging. Most of the time, the pick-offs were harmless—a ball would bounce and hit a player in the leg, or the arm, and he was out. And, if you could catch the ball, the other team lost the thrower. There were boys on our team who would thrive on attempting to catch the balls that were thrown by the other team. There were girls who would stand directly in front of an opponent and dare the thrower to try to tag them. A quick catch, and the opponent was out. These brave players would throw themselves in front of the balls, catch them, and return fire quickly to get another player out on the opposing team.

I was not one of those who thrived on catching the ball. My eye-hand coordination was not gifted on the dodge ball field, and I would find myself doing more dodging than catching. I tried, but I just did not have the mindset to stand bravely in front of an opponent as they hurled a ball at my body. I preferred to be behind those brave warriors who thought catching was the ultimate goal of the game. I did not mind allowing them the pride of victory as they wore down the opponents and picked them off one by one.

And that dodge ball mentality still works for me today. When the spiritual opponents in this life hurl balls of discouragement, pain or disillusion, I dodge. I get behind the greatest Catcher of all time, as Jesus has promised to be our shield, and the one who lifts our head. I love that phrase—when I am scared or discouraged, I tend to keep my head down. Emotionally, I am withdrawn, but He won't let me stay there. He deflects the attacks of the wicked one, and then He gently reaches down and lifts my head. He lets me know I don't need to be scared anymore—the attack is over, and He is the only One still standing. Spiritual Dodge Ball—stand behind the One who never loses.

THOUGHT-PROVOKER:

In what areas of life do we need God to defend us and lift our head? Are we allowing Him to do it, or are we taking the blows ourselves?

Dear Lord, thank You for being our shield and for lifting our heads when we are discouraged, scared, or disillusioned. Help us to stop taking the hits, and come to You, knowing You never lose. In Jesus' name, Amen.

NOTES/INSIGHTS:

WHITE WATER RAFTING

"However, when He, the Spirit of truth, has come, He will guide you into all truth; for He will not speak on His own authority, but whatever He hears He will speak; and He will tell you things to come."

John 16:13

I had my first experience white water rafting this past summer. Our group was a fifty/fifty split of first-timers and experienced rafters. Some of our group knew the river well—they had rafted it several times before, and others of us, like myself, had no clue what we were about to face. Before we could enter the rafts, we had a session on river safety and commands the guides would use. After that, we were assigned to raft seats, picked up our life jackets, paddles, and helmets and headed to the bus to go to the river.

The particular river we were on did not ease us into the trip. From the moment we were aboard the raft and shoved off, we were in moving water. I was assigned the seat next to our guide, and he knew where to point the raft to avoid the underwater rocks, and where to go to allow us to enjoy the rapids without endangering anyone on board. Regardless of our level of experience, he was able to give instructions to everyone in the boat so we did not flip the raft or get caught in tidal currents. He was an expert rafter, knew the river, and had been down the rapids many times. It gave me a sense of relief to know that the one who was ultimately piloting the boat was the one who knew the river best.

In our spiritual lives, God has given us the safety session of salvation. When we are introduced to Christ as the Savior of our souls, He gives us the life jacket of redemption and He teaches us the basics of the faith through His Word. Jesus also promised us the Holy Spirit. He is our guide through the rapids of life. Even in the midst of emotional turmoil, fast-changing life events, and rocky patches of spiritual attacks from the outside, He will steady the boat. He will guide us into all truth—not just the truth we want to hear, but the truth we need to keep us going. And He can guide a brand new Christian with lots of questions, just as well as He can lead a mature believer in the faith. He knows how to guide us through the rapids and how to lead us through the quiet spaces in between. He knows how to traverse the deepest of waters, and He will keep us from the rocks that attempt to throw us overboard, if we will follow His instructions and paddle as He directs.

Thought-provoker:

Are we yielding to the direction of the Holy Spirit, or do we think we can paddle the boat on our own? What does following the Spirit's leading look like in our lives?

Lord, thank You for the Guide You have given us to help us as we paddle through this life. Help us to yield to the Spirit's leading today and always. In Jesus' name, Amen.

Notes/Insights:

Wrestling

"Be sober, be vigilant; because your adversary the devil walks about like a roaring lion, seeking whom he may devour. Resist him, steadfast in the faith, knowing that the same sufferings are experienced by your brotherhood in the world."

1 Peter 5:8-9

Our boys have a friend who wrestled from the time he was young, until he graduated high school. Both of our sons are over six feet tall and somewhat lanky, while Caleb, their friend, is shorter, but athletically built. Sometimes when we all get together, the boys will goof off like typical young men do, and Caleb will grab one of them in a wrestler's hold. Whichever of our sons he has chosen to hold will then attempt to get out of the move, but since they are not experienced with wrestling moves, it usually winds up being a bout of laughter and jokes as Caleb will usually pick him up and then act like he is going to slam him to the mat, only to let go, joke and start again, all in fun. On one particular occasion, I laughed as I watched them and told Caleb to pick on someone his own size, to which he quipped, "You know he's bigger than me, right?"

You know, our enemy is bigger than us too, and he doesn't

fight for fun. The devil doesn't even fight fair. He will knock us down, kick us while we are down, and then pile on the discouragement to keep us from getting back up. He knows how, where and when we are vulnerable, and he has no mercy. He doesn't put us in a wrestler's move for fun on a Saturday afternoon with friends—he grabs with a chokehold and won't let go.

But, there's a second part to wrestling that is our saving grace. In wrestling, there is a move called a "tag in." When wrestling with a partner, you can tap out and allow the partner to move into the fight. Jesus is much better equipped to handle the devil and his moves. Jesus outsmarts, outmaneuvers, and defeats the devil and anything he can throw at us. When confronted directly by the devil, Jesus answered with the Word of God; He quoted Scriptures (Matthew 4). He then went to the cross and delivered the ultimate smack down on the devil (1 Corinthians 15). So, the next time your unfair, unrelenting enemy decides to target you, get behind the One who can defeat the devil any day of the week. Quote His words, speak His name, and watch Him win the day for you.

Thought-provoker:

Are we allowing Jesus, the Ultimate Victor, to fight our enemy, or are we trying to do it on our own? What do we need to do differently today to get out of the enemy's chokehold?

Dear Lord, thank You that You have defeated the devil, death, and any other enemy we have. Help us to rely on You to fight our battles by being in Your Word, and speaking Your name. We have no strength on our own, but with You, we are undefeated—to You be the glory. In Jesus' name, Amen.

Notes/Insights:

CYCLING

"Love suffers long and is kind; love does not envy; love does not parade itself, is not puffed up; does not behave rudely, does not seek its own, is not provoked, thinks no evil; does not rejoice in iniquity, but rejoices in the truth; bears all things, believes all things, hopes all things, endures all things."

1 Corinthians 13:4-7

This past year, my husband took up long distance cycling. At first, thirty miles seemed like a long way, but the longer he stuck with it, and the more he rode, the easier it became to accomplish that distance. One of the major challenges, however, is that we live in a hilly area. Thirty miles on a flat road is much different than thirty miles on a hilly one. John was describing one of these rides to me one Saturday afternoon and he said, "It doesn't matter how tired you are, or how much your muscles are complaining, if you stop pedaling on a steep hill, the bike will fall over."

The bike will fall over. Sadly, this is a picture of many relationships. When individuals and couples get into hilly territory, they call it quits. They give up on the fundamentals of pedaling, in an emotional sense, and their relationship falls over. It dies on the side of the road, because neither one wanted to keep pedaling through the pain. It's not just couples, either. Church members decide not to keep cycling through the ups and downs of loving others, and the church dies. Others decide to stop loving a difficult child, and the relationship goes dark.

But, love is a lot like cycling uphill. In spite of the discomfort, love continues to pedal. It refuses to believe the relationship is not worth the effort and, at least one person, keeps pedaling. Someone loves through the uphill climb of a communication breakdown and, instead, chooses to believe that love is not rude. A couple chooses to not take the bait in an argument, but seeks the truth and the kindness to push through the anger and frustration. Still, someone else determines to believe, hope and endure, even when the other person is silent or rebellious. The ones who pedal believe love propels us past these hills of difficulty and allows us to see the beautiful results of cresting those hills and seeing an amazing view—the panoramic view of God's love over a broken world. When things seem impossible, He will not give up. He keeps pedaling through our trials, rebellion, confusion and hurt. And He gives each of us a glimpse of His all-consuming, faithful, eternal love, each time we pedal those hills one more time and refuse to allow the bike to fall over. So today, whether you are in the flatlands of a long and comfortable relationship, or you are attempting to climb the steepest of hills, keep pedaling.

Thought-provoker:

In what areas of our lives do we need to recommit to pedaling through to keep love alive? Where are we doing well loving others? Where do we need to improve?

Dear Father, thank You that You never give up on loving us. Help each of us today to pedal through the hills, as we depend on You to give us the strength we need to keep on loving. In Jesus' name, Amen.

NOTES/INSIGHTS:

THE MOUTH GUARD

"Set a guard, O Lord, over my mouth; Keep watch over the door of my lips."

Psalm 141:3

In most contact sports, part of the uniform is a required mouth guard. Whether it is because of flying pucks, tackles, punches or body checks, protecting the mouth is part of the rules. Each one of the mouth guards has to be tailored to the player. Our friends' son plays football on the local recreation team, and they had to boil his mouthpiece, let it cool for a few seconds, and then he put it in his mouth so it would shape to his teeth and hold firm, even during collisions and tackles. The mouth guard protects their son from things on the outside. It will, hopefully, protect him from losing any teeth and minimizes injury to his mouth in case of contact. It also keeps him from biting his lip because the guard makes it nearly impossible for their son to open his mouth to allow his lip between his teeth.

What if God required each of His players to wear a mouth guard, but instead of protecting us from what is on the outside, it could protect us from what is on the inside? The Psalmist pleaded with God, on several different occasions, to put a watch over his mouth and to be sure it is the Lord's praise that comes from the his lips (Psalm 19, 34, 49, 119). In other places, he asks the Lord to keep his mouth shut in the presence of the wicked, and to shut the mouths of others when they attempt to speak lies (Psalm 36, 39, 144). What if God's guard could protect us from speaking things that would be harmful to others, that He would keep our mouths, and we wouldn't even need to bite our lips to accomplish it?

The good news is that He does provide such a mouth guard. The leading of the Holy Spirit in our lives does include what comes out of our mouths. In 2 Corinthians 10, we are told to bring every thought captive to Christ. Thoughts are the beginning of words. In Matthew 6, Jesus gives us the example of how we should pray. He tells us to ask the Father to lead us away from temptation and to deliver us from evil. This includes the words that come out of our mouths. God has given us the mouth guard of the Spirit; the challenge is whether or not we will put Him in His rightful place and allow Him to guard our mouths.

THOUGHT-PROVOKER:

Are we allowing the Holy Spirit to guard our mouths and keeping the words that come out in line with truth, mercy and grace? What steps do we need to take today to be sure our mouths are well guarded?

Lord, thank You for the Holy Spirit that is willing to guard our mouths and to keep our words sweet, pure and full of praise to You. Help us to follow Your leading today in the words we should say today. In Jesus' name, Amen.

NOTES/INSIGHTS:

KNEEBOARDING

*"For this reason I bow my knees to the Father of our Lord
Jesus Christ, from whom the whole family in heaven and
earth is named, that He would grant you, according to the
riches of His glory, to be strengthened with might through
His Spirit in the inner man."*

Ephesians 3:14-16

When our family goes out on the lake, I prefer to kneeboard. Instead of being strapped into big, bumbly skis (I am
only five foot four inches), I like to be strapped onto the board
that I can kneel on and manage better. Usually, my family
allows me to go first—most likely so they can have the rest of
the afternoon to jump wakes and do stunts, but maybe also
because I'm the mom, and we have done our best to rear them
with good manners.

The kneeboard is very different from the skis. I have to pull
myself up onto the board, while holding onto the rope, then,
I am able to get strapped in and secure. Once that is done, I
can lean back, turn different directions, even turn a complete
360 degrees. Even in rough waters, I am fine, as long as my
knees are strapped to the board.

Spiritually, prayer is very different from other spiritual exercises. Once we have been saved by God's grace, we have to make the effort to pull ourselves out of bed, out of laziness, or even busy-ness, and get ourselves settled to be able to communicate with our good and loving Father. We should desire to have that time with Him, and we make the effort to get on board.

I am not saying prayer only occurs when we are in a kneeling position, although I have found that my heart and mind need to be in a humbled position—I must push thoughts of urgency from my mind and help my heart to focus on the greatness of the One to whom I am speaking. I find when I pray first, even if life's waters are rough, I am better able to hang on for the ride. I am more secure, more settled, because I have strapped into communication with my Lord, and He is not going to let me drown. Sometimes, we even do 360 degree turns—life goes in very unexpected directions—but being strapped into my relationship with Him through prayer, He keeps me above the water and moving forward. And just like on the lake, it seems my family can have the time of their lives with God, if I pray first. So, how about we all strap in and get ready for whatever comes. We do it by praying.

Thought-provoker:

When was the last time we strapped in and settled down for a good time of communication with our heavenly Father? How about now?

Lord, thank You for the vital communication we can have with You through prayer. Help us to make the effort to find our security and peace through quiet time spent with You. In Jesus' name, Amen.

NOTES/INSIGHTS:

THE BUZZER

"In a moment, in the twinkling of an eye, at the last trumpet. For the trumpet will sound, and the dead will be raised incorruptible, and we shall be changed."

1 Corinthians 15:52

Our boys play sports with a lot of intensity. There have been occasions when a window was broken by a ping-pong paddle, uniforms had to come home in garbage bags because they were too muddy for the trunk of the car, and cleats have to be left in the bed of the truck because they were too unpleasant to smell in the cab on the way home. I love their intensity. We have done our best to teach them to balance their intensity with good sportsmanship, but that there is nothing wrong with playing their best and being focused on the goal.

In recreational sports, we didn't always have the benefit of a time clock on the field or court. We had a general idea of how long the game was going to be, but only the head referee had the exact time, and he was not always willing to share what his stopwatch said with the crowd of parents, or the players on the field. Since we didn't know, the coaches would push the boys to play strong the entire game.

Usually, the team would start out with a sense of calmness. There was a lot of passing, working around defenders and playing around at the beginning of each game. But, then, something usually changed about one-third of the way through the game. The boys began to realize they had to "pick up their game." They became more intense about their focus on the goal. They worked harder to get the ball down the field to the strikers and forwards. Their defense became more solid and they were more determined to keep the opposing team out of their end of the field. They were so focused, that sometimes the buzzer would sound right in the middle of a strong play, and the boys would look a little bewildered that the game was over.

There is a time clock on the game of life. There will be a time when God calls the game over and He calls us home. He is the only One who knows that time, and like the referee, He isn't sharing that information with us. So, we need to adopt the coaches' philosophy—play strong the entire time. If we have been calm, playing around instead of focusing, it's time to get strong. We need to witness, serve, and obey with intensity. We need to realize the buzzer could sound at any time, and rather than wishing for a better game, we should be so focused that we are surprised when He calls us home and says, "Well done."

THOUGHT-PROVOKER:

What is our intensity level? What should we do differently today knowing the buzzer of life could sound at any moment?

Dear Lord, thank You for not telling us exactly when the game will be over so that we will be more intentional about serving and witnessing for You today. May You find us faithful until the final moment. In Jesus' name, Amen.

NOTES/INSIGHTS:

THE FIELDER

"For we do not wrestle against flesh and blood, but against principalities, against powers, against the rulers of the darkness of this age, against spiritual hosts of wickedness in the heavenly places. Therefore take up the whole armor of God, that you may be able to withstand in the evil day, and having done all, to stand."

Ephesians 6:12-13

Our boys have played baseball since they were four years old. They started out with little leaguer gloves and the smallest legal bat we could find. Each year, they progressed and learned more about the game. Our oldest continued with the game, and played through high school. He had many different coaches and many different teammates. He learned different batting techniques, and how to be effective turning plays. There was one thing, however, that did not change—whenever his team was playing in the field, they were expected to get the ball and make the play.

The fielder's job is to stop the progress of the opposing team. Whether that means catching a pop fly, or fielding a ground ball and getting it to the first baseman, the fielder is to be the one who stands in the way of the other team's scoring. From the first practice, the boys' coaches would tell them to step in front of a ground ball, use your body, and keep the ball in front of you. When they were in the outfield, we'd hear the coaches say, "Make sure you see the ball and get your body underneath it." It didn't matter if they were playing infield or outfield, the fielder's job was to get to the ball and stop the other team from scoring.

On a spiritual playing field, whether we are in the outfield of foreign missions, or the infield of stateside ministry, we are to take a stand. We are to put ourselves in position to stop the opposing team's progress. In the passage from today, it says that once we have put on the entire armor of God, we are to stand. Get on the field and be a player who is engaged in the game. In verse eighteen, it goes on to say: "being watchful to this end with all perseverance and supplication for all the saints." So, whether it is the pop fly of deception, or the ground ball of deceit, we are to get in front of it by being watchful and praying for others. We are to take up a position on the field, wherever it is that our Coach sees fit to place us, and we need to make the plays. Stand fast, keep our eyes open, and pray—these are the ways we make a difference in the game.

Thought-provoker:

Are we playing our positions effectively? Are we engaged in the game? What do we need to do to be more effective today?

Dear Lord, thank You that You place us where we can be of service to You. Whether near or far away from home, help us to make the plays that stop the enemies' progress by praying for each other and standing strong in You. In Jesus' name, Amen.

NOTES/INSIGHTS:

THE TIME OUT

*"And He said to them, "Come aside by yourselves to a
deserted place and rest a while." For there were many coming
and going, and they did not even have time to eat. So they
departed to a deserted place in the boat by themselves."*

Mark 6:31-32

Almost every sport has a time out. It is a moment when the
coach, or sometimes a player, can call for a break. Or, it is part
of the game, such as a halftime, or period break. It is a time for
the team to regroup, rest, rehydrate and prepare for what is next.
Planned breaks allow players to know there will be a respite
from play and allow them to work harder, because they know
there will be opportunities to catch their breath. Other times,
however, the coach calls a timeout because he sees weariness
or discouragement on the court, and he needs time to pull his
team back together.

In life, we know our Coach plans breaks. God wisely
included holidays and Sabbaths in the Scriptures to teach us
that we need to take regular times to rest and rejuvenate. But,
then there are the timeouts. The unexpected times that God
calls us aside. Sometimes, it's a mental time out—He calls us

to readjust our expectations and conform our thinking to His Word (2 Corinthians 10). Other times, He calls a spiritual time out. He shows us an area where repentance and restoration are necessary in order for us to keep moving forward in our spiritual journey (Hebrews 12). And then there are the times, like in today's passage, He calls us to physically rest. It says the disciples were so busy ministering that they did not have time to eat. For bodies that run on physical food for fuel, this wasn't healthy. He tried to get them away in verse 31, but the crowds flocked to where they saw them going, and Jesus feeds them all. The disciples are still ministering. I wonder if they looked weary by the end of the day, because Jesus took the entire team out of the game for a time out. He put them in a boat and sent them away. The demands from the crowd were still there, but He let the disciples take a break. And through the time out, He teaches them to walk by faith.

When God calls us to time outs—either planned, or unexpected—we should look forward to the rest, and the lessons, He has planned. We shouldn't resist, we should trust our Coach and know that He has a greater plan as He makes the call—the call to rest, restoration, or rejuvenation. It's our part to take the time out.

Thought-provoker:

Is there an area in our lives that we need to accept the time out and deal with a mental, spiritual, or physical issue? Will we take the time out?

Dear Father, thank You for the time outs. Help us to look forward to them instead of thinking we don't need them. Help us deal with the issues that You want dealt with in our lives today, even if it means taking a break. In Jesus' name, Amen.

NOTES/INSIGHTS:

ZIP LINING

"And when He had come into the house, the blind men came to Him. And Jesus said to them, 'Do you believe that I am able to do this?' They said to Him, 'Yes, Lord.' Then He touched their eyes, saying, 'According to your faith let it be to you.'"

Matthew 9:28-29

Zip lining may not seem like an everyday sport, but it is a recreational sport gaining popularity all over the world. I found myself standing on a zip platform, four stories up, after having made the climb up a wooden ladder, that spiraled around at one point, to continue the climb up. I had already done one zip line, and climbed several obstacle bridges to get to this particular zip line. Four stories up is not terribly high, but it was deceptive, because we were going to zip into a forest terrain that went downhill underneath us. I knew my harness was good—I had tested it at the other obstacles on our way to this point. I knew I had made it up the ladder, and I knew all I had to do was step off the stage and I would be enjoying a zip through beautifully tree-lined landscape. But, I stood there. My friend was climbing the ladder under me and she looked up and said,

"Just go. It's fun." I said, "I know. The hardest part is the first step off the platform." She laughed. "Yep, but such is life."

I closed my eyes for a second and stepped off. The zip harness caught me and before I knew it, I was enjoying the view and feeling the breeze on my face. The anxiety of the previous moment dissolved as I zipped along toward the landing platform.

In the passage today, blind men come to Jesus and asked to be healed. They knew He could do it; they had heard the stories of His miracles. They had made the journey to find Him, and He had given them an audience to make their request. "According to your faith let it be to you." Wow. Jesus told them their healing would be based on what they believed. Did they step off the platform of faith, trusting for complete healing? What about us?

Stepping out in faith means we go all in. I couldn't enjoy the zip line and keep one foot on the platform. I had to trust the harness would hold me. We know that God has held us before; we have to trust the God of the universe will hold us when we jump into His hands and believe with everything we've got. It's then, and only then, we can enjoy the view and feel the breeze of joy on our faces.

THOUGHT-PROVOKER:

What's keeping us from stepping off the platform into full faith? What can we do to take that leap today?

Lord, thank You that Your harness of faith holds us in this life, and You will never let us fall. As we trust You more, help us to step out and show those around us what it means to live in faith, enjoying and trusting You, and feeling the joy on our faces. In Jesus' name, Amen.

NOTES/INSIGHTS:

UNIFORMS

"Behold, how good and how pleasant it is for brethren to dwell together in unity!"

Psalm 133:1

Almost every team has a uniform. Even gym classes have uniforms—a designated outfit to be worn while participating in the class or sport. It helps others to know which team one plays on, whether they are a teammate or an opponent, and it helps spectators tell the teams apart. So, what's so special about a uniform?

Uniforms promote teamwork. Those who wear the same uniform are working toward the same goals. They have the same coach. They play the same strategy. They win, and lose, games together. Friendships are forged on the fields of sports. Strangers come together, don their uniforms, and they learn to work together as a team.

Uniforms provide identity. Team members know who they can trust on the field, who is on their side, by the color of the uniform they wear. In the midst of fast breaks, quick action on the field, or times of strong defense, one player needs only to see his team's color to know the player he is passing to is going to help him toward the goal, or turn play back into their opponents' end of the court or field.

Uniforms promote camaraderie. One only needs to go

downtown for a major sporting event and the home team colors are visible everywhere. Businesses support the team by displaying the home team's uniforms and colors. Strangers will speak to each other because of the colors they are wearing. They will sit together in a stadium—sometimes thousands of them at one time—and they will cheer for the home team.

What, then, is the uniform of the believer? We are to put on the new man. We are to take on a new uniform, one that identifies us as members of the heavenly team. We put on a unique uniform that includes the fruits of the Spirit and the humility of Christ (Ephesians 4; Galatians 5). Our spiritual uniform is colored by love, pressed by self-control and bearing each other's burdens. It is sewn together with joy and peace, and it is fitted with patience and perseverance. A uniform like no other, for a team that is called from all parts of the world to become unified in our work, giving glory to our Captain, and showing the world of opponents that we can work as a team and find unity in our calling. It gives us the ability to talk to strangers, and find camaraderie in the bond of Christ. It identifies us with Christ who died for us, as we make the choice to don His uniform and be identified with Him. Our team has a uniform—let's choose to put it on and make the team today.

Thought-provoker:

Are we wearing the uniform of the heavenly team, or have we chosen to wear the world's uniform today?

Lord, thank You for the awesome opportunity to be identified as member of Your team and to wear Your uniform today. Help us to don the uniform of Christ-likeness and to be witnesses for You today. In Jesus' name, Amen.

Notes/Insights:

DIVING

"For everyone who partakes only of milk is unskilled in the word of righteousness, for he is a babe. But solid food belongs to those who are of full age, that is, those who by reason of use have their senses exercised to discern both good and evil."
Hebrews 5:13-14

Most of us enjoy at least putting a toe in the water on a hot day, but divers take this to a whole other level. They put themselves on a platform in the air above the water, take their stance, and jump into the water. There is no hesitation once they have stepped off the platform. There is no going back, wishing for the platform under their feet—they commit and they dive.

There is a learning process to diving. The divers have to start with a love for the water. If they do not enjoy the water, diving becomes a worthless effort, because they will do everything in their power to avoid getting into the pool. Diving also takes perseverance. It is tough to stand on that board or platform and know that one is deciding to make the leap. They also learn how to handle the pressure—the change of pressure as they dive from air to deep water. They know three feet of water will not stop their momentum, so they have to go deeper to be able to recover and swim back up to the surface.

Bible study and doctrine are a lot like diving. We don't expect toddlers to be able to dive off platforms; in fact, we discourage it. We want them to learn to love the water by sitting and splashing in it, or being held by a parent as they bob up and down and get used to the feel of it. But, there comes a time, after they have learned to swim, that they need to dive. They need to get out of the comfort zone of the shallow end and start learning the deep truths of the Word of God. If we keep teenagers in the shallow end, they will never know the joy of overcoming their fears and jumping off the platform. Divers understand this. They know the joy that comes with a well-done dive, and they come out of the water with smiles on their faces. But, if we never let them dive, they don't ever learn to handle the pressure or develop the technique to dive well.

As students of the Word, we need to get out of the shallow end. We need to keep moving into deeper waters of study, to wrestle with our doubts and to come to a firm belief based on the Word of God. When we do, we will look forward to the dive.

Thought-provoker:

Where are we in the diving process? Staying in the shallow end too often? Keeping others from the dive? What was the last dive we knew that brought us joy?

Lord, help us to dive deep into Your Word and to wrestle with deep truths, so we know what we believe and why we believe it. In Jesus' name, Amen.

Diving

NOTES/INSIGHTS:

THE SCOREKEEPER

"For what profit is it to a man if he gains the whole world, and loses his own soul? Or what will a man give in exchange for his soul? For the Son of Man will come in the glory of His Father with His angels, and then He will reward each according to his works."

Matthew 16:26-27

Every major sport has a scoring system, and those who keep the score. In fielding games, such as baseball and softball, the score is measured in runs and the statistics are kept on both defensive and offensive plays. Court games, such as basketball, tennis, have different scoring systems—basketball awards points based on the distance from the basket, and tennis awards a big point spread for each point earned. Football earns points based on what type of play is made to score. Field goals are awarded three points, safety plays are worth two, and touchdowns are worth six. Extra points are one each. The point is each game has a system for determining who wins the competition.

In the spiritual realm, our place on the team is secure. Jesus Christ paid the redemptive price on the cross so each of us could become a member of His team (John 1:12). As a member of the team, however, He expects us to score. There are several passages in Scripture that give us the methods for scoring on our heavenly team. We are to be unified in the body of Christ, walk in the Spirit, put on the characteristics of a Godly player, and exercise the freedom to forgive—and that is from just one chapter (Ephesians 3) in the New Testament! We are to also tell others of the grace of God, endure the rigors of the game of life, and keep our eyes on the One who has called us to be a part of His team and to play by His rules (2 Timothy 4). In doing these things, we are doing the good works that He promised to reward.

So, who is the scorekeeper? The Lord Jesus told us that we should be scoring so much, so often, that we can't keep up with the score (Matthew 6). While we may try, He is the ultimate scorekeeper. He keeps everything recorded in His books—our tears and our ways (Psalm 56). And, one day, He will test each of those works, whether or not it was done for His glory, and the things we did for Him, will survive the fire (I Corinthians 3). Today, let us be about scoring for the kingdom, and do it for Him, not for us.

THOUGHT-PROVOKER:

What kind of works are we doing each day? Are we scoring for the kingdom, or trying to make points for ourselves?

Lord, thank You that You keep the score and Your books are fair and just. Help us to score good works for Your glory, and to be doing so much good in Your name that we cannot keep score as a team, but to leave that to You. In Jesus' name, Amen.

NOTES/INSIGHTS:

ARCHERY

"Let the words of my mouth and the meditation of my heart be acceptable in Your sight, O Lord, my strength and my Redeemer."

Psalm 19:14

There are many complex bows in archery. There are compound bows that have pulleys and cables that make them powerful for hunting; and there are crossbows that actually have triggers to shoot the arrow. There are still other bows that have mechanisms that allow the bow to fall as the arrow shoots, so the bow does not interfere with the arrow's trajectory. So, when I started into archery, I was very overwhelmed. A wise, older archer (my dad) suggested I start with a recurve bow. The recurve bow is a long bow that has the ends curved back, so the pull on the string bends them and creates more power behind the arrow. It's a simpler bow to use, and an archer typically uses a recurve bow when he or she needs to learn good form and technique.

There are many types of worship promoted in the church culture today, and I do not stand in judgment that one is better than another. I know there are other spiritual archers out there who understand the ins and outs of their particular types of worship and they are able to connect with God through it. But, for some (like me), we can get overwhelmed by all the options. A wise mentor has come alongside of me at different times in my life, and she has advised me to take a step back and find the simple focus for my worship. She noticed I was trying to make it too complicated, so she turned to the passage from Psalm 19. In her advice, she said to focus on the words that were coming out of my mouth—moment by moment—not just during the times I said I was worshiping—and then I needed to check my heart. If those two things were aligned with God's Word, then my worship would be acceptable. I had to take away some of the ideas and traditions that I thought were so important—just like some archers have to deviate from the bows that their relatives use to be able to focus on their own form and technique. When I let those things go, I could then focus on the importance of pulling back the string of obedience in my life and allowing the Spirit to set the arrow's flight. Going to simple helped me. Maybe it can help us reconnect with the Lord the way that pleases Him.

THOUGHT-PROVOKER:

Are we making worship too complicated in our lives, or maybe for others around us? What can we do to reconnect with God?

Lord, thank You that You do not make worship complicated for those of us who need it to be simple. Please help us to focus on connecting with You and allowing You to guide the arrows of the different areas of our lives as we trust and obey You. In Jesus' name, Amen.

Notes/Insights:

The Gym Bags

"Also He said to them, 'Is a lamp brought to be put under a basket or under a bed? Is it not to be set on a lampstand? For there is nothing hidden which will not be revealed, nor has anything been kept secret but that it should come to light. If anyone has ears to hear, let him hear.'"

Mark 4:21-23

All of our kids play different sports. Because each of them is different in their personalities and preferences, we encouraged them to find the sports they enjoy. With each sport comes different necessities, so each of them has a bag that carries their equipment, extra clothes, sports drinks and cleats or shoes. The interesting thing about each of their bags is that each one has its own unique smell. Our oldest son's bag smells like the oil he uses on his glove. Our daughter's bag smells like leather, as her bag contains different elements she uses for horseback riding. Our middle son's bag is a unique combination of cleat leather and dirt, as he plays goalie for a local soccer team. Each one of their bags holds the things that show which sport they play. Without seeing the bag, I can tell which one left their bag in the trunk of my car by what I smell when I open the trunk door. Even in the dark, I can sense whose bag has been left in the corner of the laundry room. There is uniqueness to each one that makes it stand out from the others.

Each of us should be like a gym bag. Not that we should smell, but that we should be unique. As believers, we are to have a testimony that is different from the world's. In today's passage, Christ says there is no point in lighting a lamp and putting it under a bed. That is not the purpose of the lamp. He also says there is nothing hidden that won't be revealed. We each have the Spirit of God indwelling us as His children. We should live in such a way that it is not a secret that we are Christians. When I open the trunk of my car, there is no mistake that there is a gym bag in there. When others peek into our lives, there should be no doubt that the Holy Spirit is the One in control. Unlike the gym bags that are sometimes potent, there should be a uniqueness about us that attracts others to want to know God. Those gym bags are full of stuff that our children need to play their sports. Our lives should be full of the things that point others to God. In this way, we should all be gym bags.

THOUGHT-PROVOKER:

Are we stuffing our life-bags with junk, or are we filling it up with things that point others to God? What do we need to change to be better witnesses for Him today?

Lord, thank You for the uniqueness You've given each of us. Help us to be the testimonies we should be to point others to You. In Jesus' name, Amen.

Notes/Insights:

THE BUTTERFLY STROKE

"My brethren, let not many of you become teachers, knowing that we shall receive a stricter judgment. For we all stumble in many things. If anyone does not stumble in word, he is a perfect man, able also to bridle the whole body."

James 3:1-2

Our niece and nephew are on a swim team. They spend hours in the pool, mastering the Freestyle and the Breaststroke for their individual races and relay teams. They also have learned how to swim backwards—the Backstroke is where they propel their bodies through a lane of water while not being able to see where they are going. And then there is the Butterfly: the warrior stroke of swimming. It takes everything the swimmer has to keep the body in coordination as stroke after stroke requires them to lift up out of the water, pull themselves forward with a big arm stroke, bend their body to the next movement, hit the water and propel themselves forward again with a powerful dolphin kick. It is a competitive stroke that takes a lot of muscle memory to do well and look graceful. As their aunt, I am very proud of them and their accomplishments, but they won't see me competing at a swim meet.

Just as swimmers invest a lot of time, energy and muscle into becoming competitive at the Butterfly, teachers of the Word need to spend as much, if not more, in the spiritual pool of learning and discerning the Word of God. James tells us there is a stricter judgment for teachers. We are held to a higher standard, even though he admits in the very next sentence that we stumble in many things. Just like those swimmers who attain to master the Butterfly stroke, teachers must keep propelling themselves into deeper truths in the Word, asking God for wisdom (James 1:5) and spending time alone with God so the Spirit has the ability to remind us of truth (John 14:25-27).

But, it is so worth it. Watching those swimmers thrust themselves out of the water and propel themselves forward in grace and rhythm is amazing. And watching a teacher who has spent time with God, who has studied diligently from His Word, and is relying on the Spirit's leading, who then sits with a group of people eager to hear, is an amazing thing as well. Those who are called to swim must swim. It's deep within their personalities and their bodies gravitate toward all that is involved in doing it well. So also teachers, those called by God to share His truths and principles with others, will gravitate toward teaching, and do it well.

THOUGHT-PROVOKER:

Have we been called to teach? Are we fulfilling that calling, and doing what is required to do it well?

Lord, thank You that we can teach others when we have Your calling, Your Word and Your Spirit as our guide. Help us to be faithful to learn Your Word, so we can teach others also. And help those of us who are learning to do so with an open and willing heart so Your Word seeps into all the corners of our lives. In Jesus' name, Amen.

NOTES/INSIGHTS:

THE HOLE-IN-ONE

"And not only that, but we also glory in tribulations, know-
ing that tribulation produces perseverance; and perseverance,
character; and character, hope. Now hope does not disappoint,
because the love of God has been poured out in our hearts by
the Holy Spirit who was given to us."

Romans 5:3-5

A hole-in-one is a phenomenon in golf in which a player tees up at the top of a hole, and with one shot, their ball travels over the fairway, over any obstacles, right over the green, and straight into the hole. A few famous golfers have done it, and there were a few hole-in-ones at our family reunion, but that was on a much smaller course with their cousins, so not exactly sure if those are to be counted or not.

Once in awhile, we have hole-in-one moments. We land a job interview right out of the gate, and they offer the job on the spot. Or, we meet someone and a friendship starts at the first moment and carries throughout a lifetime. Or, perhaps, the door of opportunity swings open and we walk straight into a successful ministry that leads to a permanent vocational decision. For most of us, however, there are very few hole-in-one moments. For most of us, we live in an eighteen hole course of life in which there are many times we have to tee up, avoid obstacles, and face challenges that sometimes leave us with a triple bogey and a lingering feeling of doubt and disillusion about the game.

When these full-course moments hit us, and we wonder if we have the strength to tee it up one more time, it's good to remember that God's plan does involve tribulation and trials. Why would a good God do that to us? Why would there be moments when we feel it's futile, or even hopeless? Because He knows these are the moments when we grow. If every golfer hit a hole-in-one every time he or she came up to the tee, golf would be the most boring game in the world. Golfers would not learn how to use different clubs, work on different swings, and develop strategies to get out of roughs. It's these skills that make golf more interesting. And it's perseverance that builds our character, and our hope. We become more interesting people to know, and have a testimony that gives God the glory, when we struggle and finally make it to the green. And that character makes us better friends, husbands and wives, brothers and sisters, and family members in God's bigger picture, than if we hit every success on the short-course of life. Today, as we deal with roughs, long fairways and bogeys, do not be discouraged—He is building us into better life golfers.

THOUGHT-PROVOKER:

Will we continue to stay in the game, meet the challenges and overcome obstacles to become better people? What are our challenges today? How will we drive through them?

Lord, thank You that life is a process and not an instant. Help us to enjoy the game, learn the skills and become the character-filled witnesses You have called us to be. In Jesus name, Amen.

NOTES/INSIGHTS:

THE ZAMBONI

"If we say that we have no sin, we deceive ourselves, and the truth is not in us. If we confess our sins, He is faithful and just to forgive us our sins and to cleanse us from all unrighteousness. If we say that we have not sinned, we make Him a liar, and His word is not in us."

1 John 1:8-10

T he intermission breaks in hockey involve the Zamboni. As it makes it rounds, it scrapes away the ice that has been chipped up by the players' skates and it lays down a new layer of ice on the floor. The crowd enjoys watching the Zamboni do its work—at some arenas, they actually applaud the Zamboni as it exits the arena to let the driver know it was a job well done.

There are some interesting things to note about the Zamboni process. First of all, the Zamboni makes the surface new again. When God first reaches into our lives and redeems us, He makes us completely new again (Ephesians 2). As we move through life, however, sin chips away at the ice of our testimony; bad attitudes and bad decisions leave scars and scrapes. God's Zamboni of forgiveness takes a person with all their flaws—their chips, scars and mars—and He gives each one of us a fresh start with forgiveness. He is willing to do it over and over again, just as the Zamboni is willing to drive the ice in between each period of hockey. Knowing how life was going to affect our ice, God gave us a way to start fresh again through confession. We admit our sin to Him, and He forgives us and we start with a new surface on the ice of our testimony.

Another interesting thing is the Zamboni is driven by someone who knows how it works. If you or I got onto a Zamboni, we would have no idea how to make it move forward, backward, spray water or turn on the ice. God drives the Zamboni of forgiveness. He designed it, and He knows how it works best. He is also able to show the world His love and grace as He works forgiveness in the lives of His children. Those who do not know how the Zamboni works should not pretend to know how to transform the ice with their own ideas, or determine someone else's ice is not worth restoring. They should, instead, trust the One who knows how it all works together.

Today, we should celebrate the work of the Zamboni of grace in our lives. We should be grateful for the moments when our loving Father touches us, forgives us, and gives us a fresh start each time we confess we need it.

THOUGHT-PROVOKER:

Are we grateful for the Zamboni moments we have each had through the blood of Christ? Are we showing the world the life we have in Him?

Dear Father, thank You for the Zamboni moments You have given each of us when You transformed us with Your forgiveness. Help each of us to live differently because of the fresh starts You have given us. In Jesus' name, Amen.

NOTES/INSIGHTS:

THE CODE OF CONDUCT

"Beloved, I beg you as sojourners and pilgrims, abstain from fleshly lusts which war against the soul, having your conduct honorable among the Gentiles, that when they speak against you as evildoers, they may, by your good works which they observe, glorify God in the day of visitation."

1 Peter 2:11-12

In every sport our children have played, there has been a code of conduct that we were required to sign and to which we had to adhere. There were rules about uniforms, required practices, and how to behave and speak while at the ballpark. It did not matter if we were players or spectators, home or visiting team, we were expected to look and act a certain way so as not to embarrass our coaches and the league.

These rules were not meant to vacuum out the fun, they were actually put in place so everyone would have an enjoyable experience at the ballpark. They were there to be sure anger did not erupt into crude language, and players were easily identifiable by their uniforms. There was also a level of respect for the sport that was expected on the field, and in the stands. One might not agree with a call on the field, but out of respect for the sport, comments were kept under one's breath and good sportsmanship needed to rule the day.

Some people would call this code of conduct legalistic. They argue that the game should be played, with all its gusto and bravado, and there should not be limits on what fans can and cannot say, and what players can and cannot do. When taken to the extreme, these individuals had no problem with brawls breaking out, law enforcement needing to be called, and possibly even arrests being made.

To them, it's all part of the game. To most of the rest of us, however, these guidelines kept the game in line and made sure nothing bad could be said about the players, the spectators or the officials in our league. Instead of seeing legalism, we saw parameters, boundaries that enabled the kids to play, and the spectators to enjoy. Spiritually speaking, the parameters God has set for His children are the boundaries that make it possible for us to be good testimonies.

God doesn't require ridiculous guidelines of us—He gives us the boundaries of honorable conduct, good work ethic, respect and love for others and a quiet, peaceable life so others can recognize that we are on His team (1 Timothy 2, 1 Peter 2-3). It worked well for our ball teams—the kids played hard and respected the game, and the spectators enjoyed the opportunity to watch and cheer. We have the opportunity, today, to play in His league and honor our association with Him.

THOUGHT-PROVOKER:

Are we pushing back on the code of conduct God has set for us, or are we able to live within those boundaries for our good and His good name?

Lord, help us to remember Your code of conduct is not laws, it's a way to live in love and show others how great You are. In Jesus' name, Amen.

NOTES/INSIGHTS:

FLASHLIGHT TAG

"Indeed, the darkness shall not hide from You, but the night shines as the day; the darkness and the light are both alike to You."

Psalm 139:12

While it may not be considered an organized sport, when our children were younger, one of their favorite summertime games was to play Flashlight Tag with all the kids in our neighborhood. Word got around the neighborhood that a game was being planned for Friday night, and all the kids would gather at dusk, check their flashlights, pick someone to be "it," and then they would head off into the backyards and common areas in our neighborhood. Under the cover of darkness, they would try to hide from the tagger and work their ways back to base. We parents would take some time out to meet on the cul-de-sac and chat about the week, or sit on the porch and hear giggles coming from the bushes as kids tried to be quiet and hide.

The goal of flashlight tag is to make it back to base without the beam of the flashlight shining on you and your name being called. They would hide in flowerbeds behind bushes, lay flat on the ground next to decks or staircases, hide behind play sets, or climb trees. Of course, the tagger knew to check all these hideouts, and runners would be seen darting from place to place to avoid the tagger's light. Eventually, everyone was found, or the runners made it back to base, a new tagger was chosen, and off they went again.

When we've done something we are not proud of, we've sinned, or we've messed up, we don't want the light shining on us and our name being called. We do our best to hide and think we can make it back to base, a restored relationship with God, without coming into the light. And yet, God knows the very thing we need to get us back to base is a shining light. Psalm 139 tells us that the night shines like the day in the presence of God, so we really aren't fooling anyone, except ourselves. We can keep trying to hide in the dark, crouching behind the staircases and decks of our pride, or thinking the bushes of shame and regret will keep us hidden. Instead, we should face the light, confess our sins, and accept God's forgiveness. It's the quickest way back to a relationship with Him. The amazing thing is God leaves the decision up to us, but He won't stop seeking to restore us. He tells us He will discipline us, because of His great love for us, but He will never let us go (Hebrews 12). When faced with hiding in the darkness or facing the light—take the light. It's much better than stumbling in the dark alone.

THOUGHT-PROVOKER:

Where do we need to face the light of God's presence in our lives today and restore our relationship with Him?

Dear Father, thank You for Your light that shines into our lives and helps us back to a restored relationship with You. Help us not to hide in the dark. In Jesus' name, Amen.

NOTES/INSIGHTS:

THE SAND TRAP

"Blessed is the man who endures temptation; for when he has been approved, he will receive the crown of life which the Lord has promised to those who love Him. Let no one say when he is tempted, "I am tempted by God"; for God cannot be tempted by evil, nor does He Himself tempt anyone. But each one is tempted when he is drawn away by his own desires and enticed."

James 1:12-14

The sand trap is an obstacle placed along a fairway or green that is hazardous to the forward direction of the ball. If a ball lands in a trap, also called a bunker, the golfer then has to expend energy, and shots, to get the ball back where it is supposed to be on the fairway or green. The obstacles are designed to sabotage the player's game. They slow the golfer down and make successes on the course tougher to achieve.

In life, we create our own sand traps. When our flesh decides it wants its own selfish way, it slows down our desires for selfless service in ministry. When it demands fulfillment, we can fly straight into the sand traps of sin and destruction, from which it will take lots of energy, and shots to our reputations, to get back on the fairway of walking with God and yielding to His will. Yes, there is forgiveness and God is able to make a beautiful testimony out of even our wildest messes, but He also allows the consequences of our temptation.

In my own life, it is the sweet-tooth train. Because of a health condition, I am supposed to avoid sugary sweets, but it seems every time I set out to eat healthy, and do a better job of controlling my nutrition, the sweet tooth train shows up. There are cupcakes at a social gathering; there are homemade cookies at a family event. Instead of enjoying a once-in-awhile treat, I find myself digging a deep hole in the sand trap of indulgence. May seem like a silly example to some, but this is an area that I have had to yield to the Spirit and allow Him to strongly take the lead in my life. I don't avoid social gatherings, but I eat healthy before I go. I graciously decline most sweets, and then the trap doesn't trip me up. And, before everyone thinks I'm some super hero—I do still occasionally enjoy a limited treat—one that keeps me within the boundaries of a healthy eating plan, but allows me to enjoy some of the sweet things of life. Sand traps—we need to be aware, and we need to avoid, so we can keep swinging positively toward the goals God has given us.

THOUGHT-PROVOKER:

What sand traps are we in, or need to avoid, today? What's our plan to stay, or get back, on the fairway of God's will for us now?

Lord, thank You that You don't send us into the sand traps of life, but You are willing to help us get out. Help us to avoid temptation and be the testimonies You have called us to be for today. In Jesus' name, Amen.

Notes/Insights:

BASS FISHING

"And the King will answer and say to them, 'Assuredly, I say to you, inasmuch as you did it to one of the least of these My brethren, you did it to Me.'"

Matthew 25:40

I was at the dock at the lake park near our house a few weeks ago, enjoying a little break from the busy season that had become our family life. We had taken a Saturday afternoon to be together as a family, and we had decided to go to the lake and enjoy the end of the summer. When we arrived, we realized we were at the starting line of a bass fishing tournament. There were several flat-style speedboats with fishing equipment and fishermen aboard, and more boats waiting to unload at the boat ramp next to the dock. As I waited by the lake as my husband parked the car, one of the participants recognized an acquaintance in another boat and called out, "Where are you headed?" The other replied, "I'm going where the Big Papa is," to which several fishermen erupted in laughter. The signal was given and the boats took off for deeper waters, and nooks and crannies, to find the best fish.

The Big Papa—the big prize. The dream job, the right salary, the perfect family, the big church—all are prizes that many seem to want in our competitive society. If we are going to fish, we want to catch the biggest one out there. We don't want to waste our time with minnows and crappies—we want our effort to be rewarded; we want our fishing to be noticed, even legendary, if possible. We want to win the biggest award; we want to be the top dog. Sometimes, we want to go after the "Big Papa," when what God really wants is for us to just go where the fish are. He even warns us in Scripture to be careful of our motives as we fish (Matthew 6). He is not concerned about the biggest fish, not even the prettiest ones—He wants us to just go fish.

Maybe it's the quiet coffee shop where you humbly meet with a few college students each week and talk about their issues, or it's the play date at the park where you listen to another mom as she expresses regrets or concerns about her life. Or, maybe it's the ride to the doctor because a friend cannot drive and has an appointment. It's about being where the fish are, not always hunting down the Big Papa, that matters. It is the small, faithful things we do, when they are done in love and obedience that make our Heavenly Fisherman smile.

Thought-provoker:

What Big Papas are we chasing that are hindering our true purpose? Are we willing to serve in small ways? What changes do we need to make to our focus, and our service, starting today?

Lord, thank You that Big Papas are not required of us as we fish for men. Help us to love and serve others in small ways and be grateful. In Jesus' name, Amen.

Notes/Insights:

THE EQUIPMENT BAG

"Or do you not know that your body is the temple of the Holy Spirit who is in you, whom you have from God, and you are not your own? For you were bought at a price; therefore glorify God in your body and in your spirit, which are God's."

1 Corinthians 6:19-20

I have noticed that almost every sport has some kind of equipment bag. Tennis players have racquet bags, ball sports have ball bags, and most players bring their own equipment in some form of bag or duffel. It is interesting to me to observe the different types of bags. It seems that the bag is a reflection of the player's personality. Some have simple, functional bags with no fancy logos or colors. Others have vibrant colors, with secret pockets and the latest gadgets to make organizing their sport bag a breeze. Whatever the case, the bag carries what the player needs to be able to play the game. What I don't typically see are bags with tears and holes, or stains. It seems that the players who carry them take pride in the bag that holds their equipment. It may be a new bag, or it may be a very old one from their first year as a player, but each bag is taken care of.

When we received Jesus Christ as our Savior—the Rescuer

of our souls because of His work on the cross, we became the equipment bag. The Holy Spirit takes up residence in us, and He has promised that we have everything we need to live the Christian life as we should (2 Peter 2:1-5). We have the promises of God, the leading of the Spirit and the hope of eternity with God in our heavenly home. The bag is filled with all the things we need. So, what does the outside look like?

I am not talking about are we tall, short, round or skinny. It doesn't matter what color our eyes, skin or hair. And, I am not talking about personality changes either. Some of us are naturally quiet, others are talkative, and still others are some style in between. What I am referring to is the question: can others tell whose equipment bag we are? Can others look at our lives and see that we belong to God's team? Regardless of whether we are a simple or vibrant type, brand new to the faith, or veterans of the walk, we are all equipment bags carrying all the things necessary for the Christian life. Our lives are characterized by the care of God, and as we carry within all the blessings of being His child, we are the equipment carriers for the Gospel. I hope others can tell to which Player we belong.

Thought-provoker:

Are we living lives that reflect the promises and blessings we carry within? What can we do to be better Gospel carriers in the world today?

Dear Lord, thank You for giving us Your Spirit, and all the things we need to live godly in this world. Help each of us to share You with others and make a difference in their lives. In Jesus' name, Amen.

Notes/Insights:

NINE SQUARE

And he said, "He who showed mercy on him." Then Jesus said to him, "Go and do likewise."

Luke 10:37

Nine Square is a fun, backyard game that our teenagers at church introduced us to and we have learned to love and enjoy. My friends, Jennifer and Kristi, and I all enjoy playing, but we have a small issue with the game—we are small—short to be more accurate. You see, Nine Square is a game in which each player is trying to keep the ball from landing on the ground in his or her square. The layout for the game is a PVC frame with nine squares in it that is on raised poles. The players attempt to hit the ball into the others' squares and hit the ground, so then that player is "out" and has to return to the first square. The goal is to become king/queen in the middle square (square nine), and stay there as long as possible. When playing with our teenage and college-aged sons (who are all much taller than their mamas), the game can become quite discouraging for vertically challenged individuals like me. We don't have a prayer against a spiked ball from a six foot three college student. But, every now and then, our children will show mercy on us.

157

They will withhold on the spiked balls for a little while, and one of the "shorties" will make it into the middle. Because of their kindness, we mamas get the opportunity to move to the center of the game and enjoy the queen's square, at least for a little while.

I think it is important that everyone of us remember to show consideration, and mercy, when we compete. That does not mean that we do not try our best and compete strongly; what it does mean is that we remember that we compete with other human beings and we must be kind. Victories won by trampling on our own integrity as we treat others poorly are not wins. It is not worth the damage that happens to our own souls, and the discouragement we cause others, when we do not remember to be kind. So, in the world of Nine Square, or on the field, the court, or other areas of competition, show mercy. Be the example of good sportsmanship, consideration and kindness, even as we compete fiercely to succeed. When we do, we live out the words of Jesus as He told the lawyer, "Go and do likewise."

Thought-provoker:

In what ways can we show mercy, even in the midst of a competition? How do we "go and do likewise" on a regular basis so others see the kindness of Jesus in us?

Lord, please help each of us to keep kindness as we compete. Help us to treat others well, even as we push ourselves to be the best at what we do. Thank You for Your kindness toward us and remind us daily to "go and do likewise." In Jesus' name, Amen.

Notes/Insights:

Swim Lessons

"Be diligent to present yourself approved to God, a worker who does not need to be ashamed, rightly dividing the word of truth. But shun profane and idle babblings, for they will increase to more ungodliness."

2 Timothy 2:15-16

W e have all been there, or at least seen it happening. A young child comes to the pool with a parent, an older sibling, or maybe even a grandparent, and the little one is hesitant to go in the water. The older participant jumps in, tells the young one how good the water feels, how much fun they are having, and coaxes the little one to come to the edge of the pool. The young one stands there, with swimmy arms or a life jacket on, and they shake their head no, time and again. Then, all of a sudden, they make the leap of faith, and they jump into the arms of their protector in the water. Everyone cheers. But, what's next?

We are all so excited when someone makes the leap of faith to become a believer in God and His work on the cross. We cheer them on, encourage them one by one, but then what? We do our youth, and young Christians regardless of their age, no favors when we coax them into the waters of faith but then do not teach them to swim. When we, as a church, do not teach them the deeper skills of Bible study, doctrine, and apologetics, we have left them to doggy paddle through their spiritual experience. Just teaching them the basic Bible stories, without teaching the deeper spiritual principles of sin and its consequences, the mysteries of marriage and purity, the power of forgiveness and the supernatural strength of God's sovereignty, we leave them vulnerable to spiritual attacks from the enemy and exhaustion from the onslaught of the world and its systems.

It is so much better when we not only teach them to jump, but when we teach them to swim. When we disciple them, teach them precept upon precept, show them how to add to their faith virtue, knowledge, self-control, perseverance, godliness and brotherly kindness (2 Peter 1:5). When we teach these things, we equip them to swim through the deep waters of life and to be able to teach others also. And isn't that what we all really want? If we do the tough work of teaching the lessons, leading the Bible studies, answering their questions, living the example, then they will be able to swim on their own and coax the next generation into a powerful relationship with Christ and His Word. Are we ready to teach them to swim?

Thought-provoker:

What energy and time are we investing to teach the next generation of believers how to swim through the deep waters of life? Are we swimming those waters ourselves?

Lord, thank You that Your Word is rich with deep truths and tough things to comprehend, but You have given us Your Spirit, and each other, to learn how to swim in the deep waters of life. Help us to help each other today. In Jesus' name, Amen.

NOTES/INSIGHTS:

A FOOTBALL

"But you are a chosen generation, a royal priesthood, a holy nation, His own special people, that you may proclaim the praises of Him who called you out of darkness into His marvelous light."

1 Peter 2:9

Most team sports use some kind of ball. Those balls are usually round in shape, and though they vary in size—from a racquetball to a soccer ball—they all are designed to roll and move from player to player in some form of fashion. It's how games are played and balls are put to good use in sports. Unless we are playing American football. The football is not round, and it doesn't really roll well. In fact, if a football hits the ground, it's considered an incomplete pass, a fumble, or a dead ball.

A football is unique in many ways. Its shape makes it more conducive to long passes, as well as being able to be handed off at the line of scrimmage. It tucks into the arm of the receivers and is not easily stripped. It can be kicked long distances, and its shape helps it to slice through winds. If spiraled, a technique a quarterback uses to make the ball spin clockwise as its thrown, a football can stay straight and accurate over several yards.

Most of the world's systems are like most sports—they have a set of rules and a type of ball they use, and they stick to them. Religions are work-based systems that tell their members to be sure their good thoughts, words and actions outweigh their bad, and then hope that is enough to be rewarded with some kind of an eternal bliss. World economies say that ingenuity, power, and influence are the keys to success. Then there is Christianity. A Savior came Who offers redemption, grace, and mercy—a uniqueness that identifies His followers by love, instead of fear and failings; a system by which its adoptees are blessed with provision from a loving heavenly Father, instead of their own striving and stepping on others to make it to the top. A unique way to live—a football in the field of living—a different lifestyle that gives the world a unique glimpse into a very different way to think, relate, live and be. In a world where most are rolling toward a destiny of separation from God, we can offer them the football of hope as we live to stand out as true disciples of God, and not just blend in with those who play the world's games. Today, hand the football—the uniqueness of Christianity—to someone who needs it, by living it out and sharing it with those around us.

Thought-provoker:

Are we living our lives as a football that stands out in the world's field of play, or are we trying our best to blend in and be like others around us?

Lord, thank You that Your plan of redemption is so unique and full of love that it sticks out like a football in the field of life. Help us to be willing to be different, unique, so others see You in us. In Jesus' name, Amen.

NOTES/INSIGHTS:

THE MID-FIELDERS

"And let us not grow weary while doing good, for in due season we shall reap if we do not lose heart. Therefore, as we have opportunity, let us do good to all, especially to those who are of the household of faith."

Galatians 6:9-10

Our middle son has played several positions in soccer. He enjoys playing forward, as he gets the opportunity and the excitement of scoring goals for his team. He has also played goalie. Being the last line of defense against the opposing team has its own attraction and adrenaline. It's the position in between the forwards and the defenders—the mid-fielders— that seems to be considered the monotonous positions.

The mid-fielders have the unenviable job of feeding the ball. They rarely get an opportunity to score, and they are supposed to keep the ball from getting too far into their own territory. The main job of the mid-fielders is to make a decision as to whether their team should press up the field, or if they should drop the ball back to the defenders so they can reposition the ball and start a new attack on the other side of the field.

Many Christians feel like mid-fielders; their lives do not seem to have the adrenaline or excitement of being on the front lines of mission work, or defending their faith at home in full-time ministry. They are faithful to show up for their team—you will find them in their places, ministering. They are the prayer warriors, the Sunday School teachers, or the Small Group leaders who prepare and show up week after week. They may not see a lot of victories, and they may not realize their influence. They are the ones who love the unlovely, help the discouraged, comfort the hurting. They understand the least of these passages in Scripture, and they are the ones fulfilling those duties. They are feeding the ball to the missionaries by upholding their needs in prayer. They are helping their churches to restructure ministries so communities are reached with the true Gospel. They are the ones who need to be reminded that every part of the work of God is essential—and they need to not give up. If the mid-fielders don't play, the forwards and the defenders have no one to hold the middle. If the faithful, the unseen pray-ers, and the quiet workers of the church don't show up, ministry is lost.

Today, if you are feeling like a mid-fielder, rejoice in the fact that the Coach knows you are on the field, and you are vital to your team. Don't give up—keep doing good.

Thought-provoker:

What should we do when we feel like mid-fielders in the faith? How can we encourage others to let them know they are vital to the church, and we need everyone to work together for His glory?

Lord, thank You that each of us is a vital part of Your team and You encourage us to be faithful. Help us to appreciate each other, and our gifts that You have given, so all of the ministry gets done. In Jesus' name, Amen.

NOTES/INSIGHTS:

THE SPAR PARTNER

"Let no corrupt word proceed out of your mouth, but what is good for necessary edification, that it may impart grace to the hearers. And do not grieve the Holy Spirit of God, by whom you were sealed for the day of redemption."

Ephesians 4:29-30

In order for a boxer to get better at the sport, he or she needs a sparring partner. Someone who is willing to get into the ring and allow the boxer to work on his/her routine. The spar partner's main responsibility is to allow the other boxer to practice how to fight in the ring. Sparring is a good exercise for boxers. It helps them to learn how to handle an opponent in the ring, and to learn what works and what doesn't. Sparing becomes a problem, however, when what started out as a training session becomes a full fight. The boxer becomes too aggressive, the punches start to land harder and harder, and the session becomes a dodge and panic routine instead of an opportunity for learning.

In the Christian world, we need partners who are willing to challenge us to grow in our faith. We need spar partners who are willing to have the tough conversations about deep spiritual truths—those who are willing to engage us with doctrine, instead of just opinions and ideas. We need to be those partners who come alongside new fighters in the faith and help them to learn and grow. Scriptures clearly teach the older members of the faith are to help the younger (Titus 2). The problem occurs when we use those times as weapons to cut each other down and discourage each other. It becomes a problem when we hit too hard with spiritual truths instead of helping them to improve their fight. Sparring partners are not the enemy—they are on the same team and they engage to help us become better fighters who then engage the enemy through the power of the Spirit. So when we are asked to spar—to strengthen others in their faith-fight—make sure we do it the way God intended. We are not to land punches and show how powerful we are. We are to speak the truth in love (Ephesians 4:15), be humble (Colossians 3; Titus 3), and help others (today's passage). By edifying and building each other up, we are able to make the body stronger as a whole and to be ready to face the real enemy when he comes to devour (1 Peter 5). Instead of beating each other up, let's take on the real enemy of our faith and take back ground for the heavenly kingdom. Spar well, friends, and take the fight to the true opponent.

Thought-provoker:

Are we beating each other up, or building each other? What can we do to improve our sparring so we are ready to fight the real enemy?

Lord, thank You for the church community that helps us to learn and grow. Help us to be strong in our faith, unified, and to stand strong against our true enemies—the world, the flesh and the devil—today. In Jesus' name, Amen.

NOTES/INSIGHTS:

THE GOLF CLUB

"Not everyone who says to Me, 'Lord, Lord,' shall enter the kingdom of heaven, but he who does the will of My Father in heaven."

Matthew 7:21

My husband plays golf, but he is not an avid player. He enjoys playing a round with friends now and then, and he will even participate in a golf tournament once or twice a year. This past summer, he decided to get a new club, and I decided to go along to get it for him as a birthday present. When we got to the sport store, the associate came over and started asking questions about what the purpose was for the club, what type of handle, composition, etc., was in my husband's search. My husband, in classic John-humor, said, "I don't know, as long as it looks cool when I'm using it." We all had a good laugh and then the associate helped him find the right club for the fairway.

We have a friend, Don, however, who loves the sport. He spends his free time on the course or studying the sport. He knows the names of players, statistics from the circuit, and which courses to play for beginners to experts. He plays every week, hates when the rain drives him off the course, and even goes to an indoor driving range during the winter to make sure he keeps his swing strong and accurate.

There are many in the world today who see Christianity as a cool club. They don't really understand how it works, or that it was designed by a Master Creator who knows exactly how it should be lived. They just see that being a decent person, going to church once in awhile and hanging out with other Christians is a cool way to live. These are the ones Jesus warns about in today's passage. Just because they hang around the game, know a little bit about how to play, doesn't mean they are true players. And while it is not for us to judge (Matthew 7:1), Jesus knows their true heart.

It is also interesting in this passage that He says those who do the will of the Father will enter the Kingdom. These individuals show there is no doubt that they know God and are willing to follow Him. These are the Don's in the spiritual realm—those whose passion for the God they serve is so evident, they may not always look cool, but there is no denying they love the Savior they follow. They stick with their faith, even when it's inconvenient, when the weather is bad, or when they face adversity. For them, for us, it shouldn't be about the cool factor—it's all about our faith.

Thought-provoker:

Are we cool-club types, or true players, when it comes to our faith? How do we live out the will of the Father so there is no doubt about our true heart?

Lord, thank You for the Dons in our lives who show us what true passionate faith looks like. Please help us to be passionate in our walk with You today. In Jesus' name, Amen.

NOTES/INSIGHTS:

HORSE SHOES

"But without faith it is impossible to please Him, for he who comes to God must believe that He is, and that He is a rewarder of those who diligently seek Him."

Hebrews 11:6

The game of horseshoes is a part of my childhood. At almost every summer family gathering, the stakes were driven, the distance measured, and the shoes were thrown. Everyone seemed to want a turn at the game, except for the younger cousins who were more interested in the swimming pool. It was a right of passage in our family, when you were old enough to sling a shoe and snag a ringer.

It was interesting to watch as my cousins got old enough to play the game. When they were finally old enough to be invited to play, they were excited. But once the shoes were handed to them, and they realized they were going to have to step up and throw, they became hesitant. I did the same thing when I was allowed to play for the first time. I did not realize how much I desired to play well, to help my team win, and how much pressure I was putting on myself over a simple game, until I held that first horseshoe in my hand.

Fortunately, our family is competitive, but not extreme.

175

While each team wanted to win, the overall goal was to pass down the enjoyment of the game to the next generation, so my older relatives were encouraging and eased the pressure with humor and family antics. Some of them would throw way off target, just to make the new players feel better about a wonky throw. My uncle would throw between his legs, and another would throw with his eyes closed. These sweet memories of others' encouragement are still ingrained in my childhood heart today. But, there still came a moment when it was my turn to throw the shoe. My dad's advice, "You can't ring it, if you don't throw it." So, I threw. Not a ringer the first time, but close.

In our Christian walk, we won't know what amazing things God has planned for us, if we don't step up and throw that shoe of faith. If we keep holding on, if we get hesitant, we won't hit the ringer. Even when we throw, we aren't always guaranteed a ringer, but we are guaranteed God will be pleased with our faith. We may not reach our own expectations, or fulfill our definition of success, but we have the peace of knowing we pleased Him with our willingness to try. And others are there to encourage us along the way. Step up and throw—you might be very surprised with how God puts it all together, and what sweet memories you will make along the way.

THOUGHT-PROVOKER:

Are we holding onto the faith shoes, or are we letting them fly and trusting God with the results? What shoes do we need to throw today?

Lord, thank You that You are pleased with our faith, and we can trust the results with You. Help us to step up and throw our shoes of faith, and to trust You with the outcome. In Jesus' name, Amen.

Notes/Insights:

TEAM PHOTO

"Brethren, if a man is overtaken in any trespass, you who are spiritual restore such a one in a spirit of gentleness, considering yourself lest you also be tempted. Bear one another's burdens, and so fulfill the law of Christ. For if anyone thinks himself to be something, when he is nothing, he deceives himself. But let each one examine his own work, and then he will have rejoicing in himself alone, and not in another. For each one shall bear his own load."

Galatians 6:1-5

We have a photo from every team on which our children have played. Whether they were formal pictures taken by professionals on Photo Day, or candid shots taken by parents from the sidelines, we have pictures. Each photo a reminder of the players, coaches and team staff who came alongside of our children and helped them in their sports.

Paul gives us a glimpse of a team photo in Galatians 6. He tells the strong players to help the weaker ones, and to be careful not to get sidetracked. He shares that each of us are to help each other—the team bears the burden together, not alone. Then, he almost seems to contradict himself in the next section, telling each of us to bear our own load. How does this work?

As a team photo represents, each person has a place on the team. Each player has a specific job to do—their own load to carry. Not everyone is the captain, and no one can play all the positions on the field at the same time. Each one fills a post on the team and contributes their gifts and talents. Then, the players come together as a team, and they can share a bigger burden, spread over many shoulders. I like to think of this as each player has a position to play, and as each one does that job, the burden of winning the victory is spread over the entire team.

There is another team aspect in the first part of the passage. Those who are strong in their spiritual walk are told to gently restore one who is overtaken. When we see another team member down and out, or injured, we can come alongside and help them to the bench, where God can apply healing and instruction. It's not in the team's best interest to leave the injured or distraught player lying on the court or out on the field. We throw their arms around our shoulders and we help them to the sideline where they can get help. We stick together as a team, and we go out on the field and do our jobs to get the victory won. Each team picture represents that process, those relationships and those victories. We don't do it alone.

Thought-provoker:

What does our team picture look like right now? Are we taking care of each other, or are we leaving injured players on the field?

Lord, thank You that our team photo includes all of us who are on Your team. Help us to work together, to restore each other, to carry our own load, and to bear the burden as a team. Together, we give You glory. Thank You for the victory. In Jesus' name, Amen.

NOTES/INSIGHTS:

ABOUT THE AUTHOR

Tammy Chandler is a wife, mother, teacher, friend, author and public speaker. She accepted Christ as Savior when she was five years old, dedicated her life to full-time service as a teenager and has worked in various ministries for the past twenty years. She has a bachelor of education degree from Clearwater Christian College, and a master of education from Jones International University. After many years of using everyday objects to teach children and teenagers, God allowed her to write *Devotions from Everyday Things* (Westbow Press), its follow-up, *More Devotions from Everyday Things*, *Devotions from Everyday Things: Horse and Farm Edition*, *Devotions from Everyday Jobs*, and now *Devotions from Everyday Sports* to include a larger audience.

When she is not writing, Tammy enjoys spending time with her husband, John, watching their sons play sports, going horseback riding with their daughter, or playing fetch with their dog, Ava. The Chandlers live in Tennessee.

Visit Tammy online at:

www.simplydevotions.wordpress.com

Also Available From

WORDCRAFTS PRESS

PONDERING(S)
Wayne Berry

WIVES BEHIND THE BLUE
Monica Amor

AN INTROSPECTIVE JOURNEY: A MEMOIR OF LIVING WITH ALZHEIMER'S
Paula Sarver

MORNING MIST: STORIES FROM THE WATER'S EDGE
Barbie Loflin

SURVIVING PITFALLS ON THE PATH
Beverly Clopton

WordCrafts.net

Made in the USA
Columbia, SC
30 March 2019